Survivalist Kung Fu

A Comprehensive Guide to Recognizing, Analyzing, and
Overcoming Real-Life Crises

Survivalist Kung Fu

A Comprehensive Guide to Recognizing, Analyzing, and
Overcoming Real-Life Crises

by
Noah Knapp

Turtle Press   Santa Fe, NM

To contact the author or to order additional copies of this book:
Turtle Press
PO Box 34010
Santa Fe NM 87594-4010
1-800-778-8785
www.TurtlePress.com

ISBN 9781934903261
LCCN 2011012748
Printed in the United States of America

10 9 8 7 6 5 4 3 2 1 0

Library of Congress Cataloguing in Publication Data

Knapp, Noah.
 Survivalist kung fu : a comprehensive guide to recognizing, analyzing, and overcoming real-life crises / by Noah Knapp.
    p. cm.
 ISBN 978-1-934903-26-1
 1. Kung fu. 2. Self-defense. I. Title.
 GV1114.7.K64 2011
 796.815'9--dc22
                        2011012748

Contents

Chapter 5: Weapons and Other Variables   76

Chapter 6: Resuming and Resetting: 104

Chapter 7: Prioritizing your Defense & Escaping the Crisis   147

Chapter 8: Practical Escape Training Drills and Preparation   163

The author would like to extend his special thanks to:

Dan Biales
For his friendship, insight, and the influential push in the right direction.

Randy, Patty, Alex, & Andrew Harris
For the honor of allowing me to find the most loyal family that I could devote myself to.

Randall Harris
A second and much due thanks to a truly wonderful friend. I can only say that my appreciation and respect is immeasurable.

David "Shoe" Gilroy
I did not truly know what it was to be proud of someone was until I met him and now "proud" is too small of a word.

Danny Raymond
Truly one of the greatest men I have ever known. His kindness is a constant inspiration.

Master Kishore Hiranand
For all the fun, laughs, and for sharing so much enjoyment of Kung fu.

Donte Neil
For all of his enthusiasm and willingness to help.

Gabriel Torres
For being so eager to lend a hand when it was most needed.

Aaliyah Wiley
The strongest person I know and for whom my respect knows no bounds.

Jango Bento
For his dedication, friendship, and for the endless generosity of his heart.

John Garcia
For the kind and eager willingness to assist.
&

Sifu Brian Knapp
For giving me the chance to do what I love and for making me appreciate my every day in Kung Fu.

Introduction

Confrontations, conflicts, and threats to our physical safety occur every day. Though each encounter may be different in size or shape, the goal for each always remains the same, to remove ourselves from the danger that threatens us. Unfortunately, it is very easy and common to lose sight of this primary objective and instead allow oneself to be confused with the circumstances surrounding an assault. However, this does not need to be the case.

Let us begin by stating that this is a book of strategy, and evasion of bodily harm is the chief aim. The techniques within are intended and deliberate in their inclusion; their purpose is to aid in the safe removal of oneself during a hostile situation. This is not to say however that the techniques contained in each section are of a lesser brand of self-defense, quite the contrary. Though falsely imbued with an image of active violence, there are many movements and techniques in numerous martial arts based entirely off of fleeing the site of an attack. Indeed, the truth cannot be denied that the primary purpose of kung fu is for self-protection.

It is important to have your priorities well in place during a confrontation. You must throw your thoughts forward in mind of success and contemplate the definition of *winning* to truly understand your goal. Everyone must then ask themselves to what end their actions will propel them. It is imperative that you realize now that physical wellbeing, made unsafe by foolhardy actions, nullifies each and every future aspiration of success. It is equally important to realize that there are very, very few situations in which one cannot simply remove oneself from a hostile environment and then entirely cancel out the danger.

Though it may seem necessary to control the situation that you find yourself in, you must consider yourself to the furthest extent of your most required intention, **to get out alive**. By needlessly accepting yourself into an aggressor's action, you have let someone else take control of that goal and put yourself at pointless risk. If a life-threatening altercation can be avoided, it is best to do so, *at all costs*.

Though myself a great advocate for always acting with honor, it is impossible to see someone needlessly remaining in a possibly life-threatening environment as noble. Consider the flawed logic of engaging or even remaining present during a conflict when safety can be assured simply by removing oneself. It is extremely important to consider that there is no "winning" a hostile encounter in which you do not wish to be a participant. In all honesty, the best you can hope for is to avoid the confrontation altogether.

Unfortunately, popular culture and foolish pride have instilled in us the need to stay in the conflict and conquer it. However, this "need" presents us with a situation of peril that is not at all worth the gamble of what we are placing at risk. Regardless of environment, what your attacker both desires and requires, is for you to remain. To better explain, let us analyze two separate types of aggressors.

Firstly, there is a known attacker, one who will utilize whatever victimization or manipulation is necessary to secure their aim. Whether by antagonizing, intimidating, or fear-mongering, it should be realized that there is no purpose in attempting to find a greater opinion of ourselves by subjecting our own self worth to any who would think less of us for seeking self-protection. Even the contrary presents a similar pitfall and is a ready subject for the alternate style of attack.

Secondly, there is assault from a stranger, a person or persons unknown to us meaning to do us harm. When confronted, many consider that there are several reasons to remain within a conflict, however, none of those considerations are valid. Curiosity or the need to understand what may have placed us in this situation might consume us. Just as well, it is best to remember that you cannot make such a situation "right." Any circumstance in which your safety is at risk is one that is automatically flawed by design.

It is well understood that the same emotions that arise during a random attack occur just as regularly as they do with a known attacker. The false idea of resistance, "They're not going to beat me" or "I'm not going to be a victim" may still crop up, in notions of refusal to be overtaken. Regrettably, these thoughts are contradictions in their attempted application. To stay is to give the aggressor what they want. To remove yourself is to remove what they desire most.

The old adage of there being a fine line between bravery and stupidity is never more true than when it comes to your own life. Imagine what purpose could be so great that you would willingly place your own physical wellbeing in peril. Protecting yourself by means of escape is not cowardice, it is intelligence and properly preparing yourself for these crises is the greatest form of self-preservation.

The instruction within this book is designed to help you identify, analyze, and safely react to any and all crisis situations that might occur. Within each chapter are specialized outlines that recognize the different variables that may arise during an attack. Once considered as a whole, this manual will provide you with the tools you will need to fulfill your one purpose during a crisis, to escape.

Once again, this book will not tell you how to conquer a bully's persistent aggressions, nor will it aid you in achieving foolish, pride-ridden delusions of "Rambo-esque" glory. It is designed solely to assist in the escape of an immediate, life-threatening situation.

Chapter 1

Your Environment Part 1: Avoidance of Crisis

There is an old martial arts adage that states, "The best way to stop a strike is not to block, but rather not to be in its path." In other words, an ounce of prevention is worth a pound of cure. This truth could not be more relevant than it is for survivalist tactics. If we simply recognize proactive safety practices, we will remove most of the danger that might confront us.

Anyone who tells you that Kung Fu is about fighting or that martial arts are all hand-to-hand combat is a fool. One of the greatest tools that any martial artist possesses is the ability to avoid the confrontation before it can occur or to defuse a situation before it can come to fruition. Avoidance of a crisis is an approach to survivalist tactics that must be respected. The utilization of hand-to-hand combat is what you do ONLY when, for some unforeseen reason, your best measures to avoid trouble have failed.

Following in this chapter are several of those preferred practices in which you can properly maintain your wellbeing without the need of engaging the attacker. Your approach to the following information should be that you are giving yourself the best possible chance for success. Even a mere attempt to perform these methods will increase your safety as well as offer you the opportunity to properly mentally prepare yourself for a crisis.

Remember at all times that your preventive preparation does not have to be difficult. In fact, even the simplest of measures can make the largest difference in your personal wellbeing. The very observance of the following techniques will make routine your safety and allow your interpretation of a crisis almost second nature. The idea is that if you can teach yourself what *not to do*, you may never need to know what *to do* upon the occurrence of a crisis.

Spot Checking Your Surroundings

Not everyone has a gun and not everyone is trying to attack you. In certain circles this type of *always prepared* thinking is called being "Kung fu crazy," but remember that paranoia is just as much a detriment to your wellbeing as being oblivious to your surroundings. To see peril everywhere is to camouflage possible real danger with a myriad of false and needless fears. Instead, use the tools you will learn in this book and your own common sense to recognize real danger when and where it exists.

First, take a look around you and see if anything looks out of place. If you see a blind corner or an entryway that you feel a bit wary about—perhaps someone might be lurking there—you can easily add to your personal safety by simply walking wide around the area in question. By even partially avoiding certain problematic hot spots you can grant yourself the few seconds that may make the difference during an attack. The small number of feet you add between yourself and the area of concern can grant you advanced notice if someone is indeed there and even these few seconds will seem like a lifetime during an attack.

Also, while looking directly for danger is important, you might not want to look completely paranoid by always checking over your shoulder. As a substitute for constantly turning about to see if anyone is following, it is instead a very useful tactic to utilize the effects of your environment for your own advantage. Take brief moments to look for shadows behind you or at reflections in the windows you may be passing by on the street. Advanced sightings of attacks can be found all around you.

The Risky, but Quicker Route

It is one thing to know how to get out of a burning building. It is another thing entirely to know not to walk into one in the first place. This example may seem simplistic, but it is amazing the dangers that we allow ourselves to become part of every day. It is often said that no one thinks it's going to happen to them, not in their neighborhood, or not that close to their work. Crises can happen to anyone at any time and "*only running to the store*" is not a valid reason for putting yourself in peril. Short cuts through alleyways, vacant lots, etc. may be a quicker path to your destination, but they can also place you at an unnecessary risk. Attackers, muggers, and other assailants tend to like anonymity and closed off areas such as the above provide them with exactly that. Though it may be quicker, these pathways provide us with a level of possible danger that cannot be justified. Higher traffic areas provide witnesses and Samaritans who might come to your aid, not to add the many additional avenues for escape.

Trouble Spots

Just as the previously listed quicker routes, trouble spots include any areas that might be problematic for escape should a crisis occur. If possible, do not place yourself in an environment where your escape is entirely dependent on only one path. Inner city, urban areas provide ample close-sided buildings that have sealed off entryways in one-sided alleys, as well as locked or "dead doors."

Scanning for Possible Persons of Interest

It is not only the physical factors of your environment that may cause you to feel unsettled. Regardless of place, it may indeed be those persons surrounding you that are raising your alarm. Certain characteristics of people seem to set us back because the statistics that surround personal attacks do not lie. Over ¾ of all violent attacks (murders, rapes, robbery, etc.) are performed by men over the age of 18, peaking at 25-29 years of age. Data points show that most attacks are perpetrated in larger metropolitan areas and performed predominantly by Caucasians. **However, this does not in any way mean that these are the only persons with whom you should concern yourself.**

True, chances are that a shorter, young girl who keeps staring at you as she walks by is not as much of a risk as the six-foot tall, 200 lb, shady stranger hiding his eyes, but **do not** allow yourself to improperly profile your possible attackers. Remember that regardless of their seemingly apparent appearance, she could have a gun and he could just be shy.

Attempting to categorize possible assailants by age, race, or assumed economic status is a flawed practice and these tactics have proven time and time again to be unreliable and may indeed allow us to blind ourselves to real dangers. People of each and every age group, race, and sex has performed a violent crime, therefore it is more important to center our attention upon the traits of the persons themselves rather than there assumed association with any "dangerous" grouping.

Certain things that you should make yourself aware of are the following:

1. Persons repeatedly staring and removing eye contact once the stare is returned.

2. Persons appearing overly anxious in some way or having nervous energy (remaining in one place while shaking or twitching an extremity).

3. Persons who appear to be out of place to their surroundings.

4. Persons obviously trying to minimize or conceal their presence.

5. Persons repeatedly scanning their surroundings.

6. Persons dressed in bulky or excessively loose clothing, wearing clothing inappropriate for climate, or clothing inappropriate for interior temperature (possible weaponry may be present).

7. Persons who repeatedly check their pockets (possible weaponry may be present).

8. Persons hiding their hands behind an object, themselves, or a possible accomplice (possible weaponry may be present)

9. Persons who readjust their position based upon your own movement (staying purposely to your sides or back, withholding themselves from standing face front).

10. Persons who cease their movement upon instances in which your own stops.

11. Persons seeming to follow you for an extended period of time.

12. Multiple persons, obviously associated, who do not remain together in a close grouping, whether moving or not.

The last observance is mentioned for a reason. You should always try to be aware of the people surrounding you, but not to concentrate on one person, thus losing your clear overview of the situation itself. Many robberies and assaults take place with multiple persons. Once any person of interest is identified, take note of their presence, and then immediately continue to scan your area for other possible concerns. The potential numerous areas of concern may seem overwhelming when looked at in a list such as the previous, but once you are actually utilizing this practice, you will notice that it is not so much that you are forced to awareness of every possibility, but rather only that you will have the ability to notice something that seems out of place.

Trusting Your Gut

Last and certainly not least: If it feels wrong, don't do it. Once again, this is not to say to fear everything and see danger everywhere, but subconsciously you may have been made aware of something that sets off alarm bells. What if you did see something? If needs be, ask yourself why you don't feel right about proceeding to a certain area. Analyze what about it is raising worry in your mind. The simple answer is, don't regret something you knew not to do in the first place.

Chapter Summary

Never forget what matters most, your safety. Far too many times, well-trained individuals, knowing better, have allowed themselves to be motivated by fear of embarrassment. Even in needing to feel respect, you must consider why you would allow yourself to hold your esteem in the hand of someone who is trying to do you bodily harm. Don't be afraid to look ridiculous. Laying in a hospital bed or coffin is much worse. Safety must come before pride.

As a balance-point, it is also important not to force yourself into seeing dangers everywhere. Unfortunately and quite often, we see threats where they do not actually exist. Yes, it is far better to look like a fool ten times than be caught in a crisis situation even once, but to let yourself find peril at every turn, you consent to blinding yourself with inconsequential factors of your environment. To even permit yourself for a moment to concentrate upon false suspicions, you may lose what edge you may have at the onset of an actually perilous situation.

While it is important to always be prepared, concede to yourself that there is not a knife-wielding man lurking behind every dark corner. Crises should be dealt with when they are present, not when they are imagined. Your training should leave you ready, but relaxed. Consider your preparedness to the following analogy of a guitar string. If you don't wind it enough, it won't play, but if you wind it too tight, the cord will break. A well-balanced awareness allows us to see potential risks without the need of constantly and actively "looking" for them.

Chapter 2

Your Environment Part 2: Recognizing and Analyzing a Crisis Situation

It is an unfortunate truth that not every crisis can be avoided. Once assured of the onset of a conflict, it is time to accept the situation and move forward. It seems ridiculous to say, "Don't panic." Panic is an emotional state that cannot be removed by want. However, it can and should be controlled. Try to realize that the crisis is a time-limited event. Regardless of what happens, the situation itself will pass. This type of removed thinking should allow you to contemplate your actions more clearly. Also, try not to forget that the circumstances are best handled systematically, and done so knowing that, regardless of outcome, you have given yourself the best possible chance for success. Following are a few guidelines that should always be observed.

Rule 1. **First of all, in a crisis, don't borrow trouble.** Try to think of the physical techniques in martial arts only as something you should consider as a fallback option since the level of immediate threat may be less than you might believe. Before you think of engaging your opponent, consider that it may be entirely possible to nullify the situation. Keep your mind open to seeing the whole picture instead of just the aggression.

Rule 2. **Do not despair if an immediate exit cannot be found.** Even if all you see are restrictions and obstacles in your surroundings, these very same limitations exist for your attacker as well. Also, consider that you can utilize these restrictions instead of fearing them. By simply manipulating your environment, perhaps by repositioning any random moveable object in the path of the attacker, you may be able to avoid the physical attack altogether.

Furthermore, and more to the point of avoidance, consider how many times people walk into a building toward an office and refuse to see the environment surrounding them. Dangers occur in the everyday and a brief glance may reveal a previously unseen staircase or an emergency evacuation chart hanging on the wall. Always keep your mind open to multiple avenues of escape. These small moments can be lifesavers during a crisis and it is not that these options need to be thoroughly studied, they need only be observed. Yes, it is true that some well-trained fighters could face ten attackers at their doorstep and still make it out of the situation alive, but wouldn't it just be smarter not to open the door in the first place? The point is that several options, other than engaging your attacker, may exist, even if your immediate and easy escape cannot be secured.

Rule 3. **Keep your mind only to the trouble that is present.** It is imperative that you deal with the immediate situation at hand. Worrying about the after-effects of your safety is a fruitless practice. If you allow yourself to be consumed with future considerations, you lose sight of your present perils. If you don't overcome phase 1 of your escape, you may never get to phase 2.

You should remember that this is not to say that no consideration should be made for what happens next, quite the contrary. It means only that the balance of your effort needs to be spent on securing you immediate safety. If said protection cannot be maintained, future wellbeing will not matter.

Assuring the Attack & Primary Preventative Steps

Not all attacks are immediately obvious to the victim. Sadly, some take time to build to fruition. To start, if you feel that you are present within a crisis situation, leave the site immediately. If you can achieve your exit free of restriction, but are still unsure of the aggression's cessation, such as finding yourself possibly being followed, confirm you are being followed by creating several angles in your path as you go. The idea is to create sight gaps that will make it difficult for any aggressors to trail you (outlined further in *Chapter 7: Prioritizing your Defense & Escaping the Crisis*). If nothing else, taking an erratic route will confirm your suspicions in that it would be unexplainable should anyone else follow such a path.

Unfortunately, simply knowing that your safety is in peril does not rid you of the threat. You must always have a goal in mind to assure your wellbeing: Remove yourself from the danger and continue toward that goal as fast as possible until you are assured of your absolute safety.

Scanning the Area of Attack

It is a wonderful thing if you can successfully flee, but unfortunately, not all crises can be escaped so easily and having to directly face the situation may be required. Upon the verification and onset of a crisis situation, surveying your surroundings during an attack is not only a smart tactic, it is a necessity. Besides holding true the possibility of multiple assailants, other unforeseen perils may exist. If you are engaged before you can safely escape a crisis situation, consider that hazards to your escape may exist by additional, seemingly non-threatening means, such as environmental constraints, random non-aggressive persons, etc. Each and any of these limitations may pose a risk to your evasion of the situation, however these and indeed all other restrictions are to be dealt with in the same manner as the assailant; nothing more than obstacles that need to be overcome.

A wonderful method for properly recognizing arrangement is to picture the drawing of a clock on the ground, placing yourself to stand in the center facing twelve. Each point is labeled with a number as in the following picture.

Immediate/Extended Overview

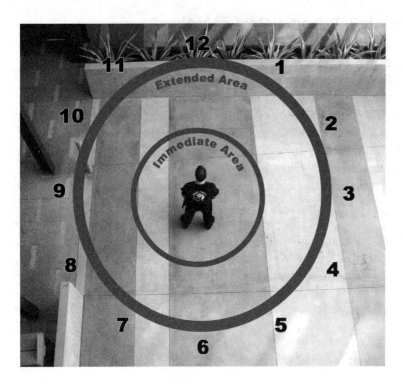

Your immediate area (outlined in detail in Chapter 3) is defined by the limit to which your reach is extended to its furthest extent. The extended area is usually defined as the space within 15-20 feet in all directions, or the size and area of a standard room.

Remember that sufficient evaluation of your situation can and should be achieved in a single moment. Once your limitations are appraised, you may choose your appropriate course of action. Proper usage of this system requires that you should consider not only the area surrounding yourself, but your opponent's as well. One quick scan of the area before the altercation has begun and you should have gained the knowledge of not only your own, but your opponent's liabilities as well.

Once your assessment of the surrounding area has been established, it is important also to take a brief moment to view those persons involved with the attack. Ask yourself a myriad of questions. Is there a possibly concealed weapon upon the attacker? Do they appear injured in some way, perhaps restricting their mobility or even limiting certain types of possible attacks they may force upon you? Does the attacker curb his movement, possibly to control and impede the sole means of your escape? Any of these pieces of information will prove vital when choosing your best possible tactics.

Immediate Threat vs. Impending Threat

Figuring out what is going to happen first during a crisis is not as hard as one would think. It is true that you may feel that you have little time to consider your best path during a confrontation, but if you take a systematic approach to ensuring the safeguard of your wellbeing, you will greatly increase your chances of success.

The easiest answer is to identify what is causing you the greatest and most imminent risk. Yes, the threats may be multiple, but they are not always equal. You must allow yourself to prioritize the danger to your wellbeing based off of the level of hazard they will impose upon you. Consider standing on the tracks of an oncoming train. It doesn't really matter if there is knife-wielding attacker running toward you from 100 feet away if the speeding train is only a fraction that distance from hitting you. Getting off of the tracks is the most important thing for you and nothing else matters if you cannot secure that end. You must pay the most heed to those dangers that are the most immediate threat before you can even think of handling the others.

Proximity plays one of the biggest parts of realizing impending vs. immediate threats. Using the recognition you have already been taught with the immediate vs. extended areas that surround you, you can now realize how to use that information to your best benefit. Identify the risks, categorize their priority, and proceed.

Immediate/Extended Area Overview

As you can see in this picture, though the threat of both men to is present, the man standing at the 12 o'clock position can represent a much higher priority hazard due to his closer proximity.

Chapter Summary

Once the situation has been assessed properly, it will be time to act. Things may seem grave, but remember that the situation is already bad enough without allowing yourself to make it worse. Focus your attentions where they belong and only where they belong, on your safety. A thousand scenarios can occur and concentrating on all of them will leave you with wasted opportunities to push on toward your wellbeing.

The answer: Don't try to solve the situation, just leave it. Discussion is worthless and reasoning is pointless considering that a violent attack is an act totally unreasonable. This is not to say that settling the situation is impossible, it is merely to declare that the odds are stacked against it and wasted resolution efforts could be better spent on escape.

The situation might seem overwhelming at first and it may seem as if the world has mounted against you, but try not to see your surroundings as a sea of endless limitations and dangers. Yes, the attacker may have placed you into an uncomfortable and perilous setting, but there is one advantage that you hold over the crisis and that one fact should be remembered above all: Your attacker has an objective that requires your presence, whether the involvement be willing or not. You, on the other hand, do not share this need. In other words, an assailant must consider holding you to the scene AND leveling and attack. You need only turn your mind to thoughts of escape instead of defeating the assailant and their goal is in ruins.

For example, consider if you can tell what direction they are trying to lead you to or pin you to? Is that a bad thing for your aim? Are they trying to keep you from one possible line of escape where they could not maintain control over you? If you don't immediately see a safe course of action, just keep moving. This will change the dynamic and possibly reveal yet unseen avenues of escape.

Even in the worst case scenario, if you can't escape, you may still find another way to ensure your safety. Remember your goal: getting to a populated area quickly. And what if, for whatever reason, this is not attainable? Remember the old saying, "If you cannot bring Mohammed to the mountain, bring the mountain to Mohammed." In other words, can you bring the populated area to you? Though it should only be done in an absolute matter of **grave** threat to you, simply pulling a fire alarm or calling 911 will bring quite a crowd to your position. Keep an open mind to your possibilities and they will increase dramatically.

Chapter 3

Manipulating the Attack and Preemptive Movements

As was stated before, not every situation can be escaped before the actual assailment takes place. Sometimes the attack is unseen until the very moment of realization, sometimes you simply cannot find a viable means of escape, and sometimes all of your best efforts to avoid a conflict fail. Regardless of the cause of onset, instances do exist that will not allow you to simply choose the path of non-confrontational escape and you will be required to accept the aggressive situation at hand.

Once the situation has been acknowledged it is time to utilize proactive safety measures that will lead to escape. Just as you are limited by your environment, so too will your attacker. By understanding the possible movements of both yourself and your attacker you should be able to predict any and all aggressive actions.

Common Mistakes Not to Make

First things must come first. You must know what NOT to do when engaging an opponent. Basic mistakes in a fight are like little holes in the window of an airplane, they may seem small, but they can quickly lead to certain disaster. Simple martial arts preparation can ready you sufficiently for your attack, but the standard rules that span across many styles can also protect you from these common mistakes.

1. NEVER PLAN MOVES IN A FIGHT.

This is one of the most common and misinterpreted topics among inexperienced fighters. It is true that to think several steps in advance during a conflict is a good practice. However, to choose in advance any specific action for yourself, whether defensive or offensive, before a situation arises may offer an attacker the benefit of success upon **every other technique** that you have not prepared. The situation itself MUST dictate the response.

Deciding on a course of action prior to the moment of contact may lead a person to make a myriad of mistakes, such as telegraphing a strike, opening guard prematurely, etc.

2. Consider that your technique could be unsuccessful.

At the point of conflict, it is important to never, never, never assume that your technique will work perfectly and without issue. Train yourself to see where you are vulnerable during a strike or a block, have a back up plan ready, and never perform a movement that will further impair your safety should it fail. Another way of thinking about it is to presume that your move will not work and be happily surprised when it doesn't. Remember the old adage: It is best to prepare for the worst and hope for the best. Observe the following two paired sequences. As you will see, by assuming a movement has a chance to fail, the intended victim of the attack is prepared for what will come next.

Move Performed Without Back up Plan   ## Move Performed With Back up Plan

The attacker squares off with you.

The attacker squares off with you.

A punch is thrown that the attacker ducks under.

A punch is thrown that the attacker ducks under.

Without maintaining a blocking hand, the attacker easily lands a devastating strike to the body.

While maintaining a blocking hand, the attacker's attempt to land a body shot is averted.

No continuing movements available

Unfortunately, after accepting such a strike, the immediate continuation of further attempts is not possible.

While assuming the strike could fail, measures were taken to allow for for new possibilities to present themselves.

3. Do not occupy both of your hands when one hand will do the job.

A fabulous method to successfully manipulate your opponent is to check both of their hands with a single on of your own. This being true, it is important to make sure that we prevent ourselves from offering this very manipulation to an attacker. It is imperative to remember that we must deal with the whole situation of an assault. One strike is not the limit of an assailant's arsenal. To use two hands to grab onto a punch, we neglect to prepare ourselves for other, now unstoppable attacks. If an attack is thrown toward you, make certain to expend the least amount of your resources (arms and legs) so that you may leave the rest free to defend yourself from other possible attacks.

Double Hand Block Occupation

The attacker squares off with you.

Both hands are used to block a strike. ▌

Single Hand Blocking Occupation

The attacker squares off with you. ▌

A single hand is used to block a strike.

With both hands occupied, the attacker easily lands a second attempt.

With one hand still remaining free the attacker's second attempt is easily averted.

4. Do not let anyone get directly to your back.

This rule may seem simplistic, but the importance of it cannot be stressed enough. Yes, the easy answer is that you just can't see where your attacker is, but once we delve into the actual positioning, we can see many more colossal perils waiting.

Consider why kung fu training focuses on squaring shoulders to an opponent instead of turning them to the side. Many martial arts would teach you to rotate your shoulders to the side so as to protect your centerline (the focused area directly leading from the top you your head to your groin, including your eyes, nose, throat, heart, diaphragm, and genitals.) The reason most commonly given for this practice is to spin these targets to the side, removing them from easy access, and offering only lesser targets such as your shoulder to an attacker. Sadly, while this looks seemingly reasonable on paper, the real-life fighting applications of this technique are completely implausible.

True conflicts are not at all like point-fighting tournaments and it is an absolute truth that attacks will not come only from the front. Strikes appear from all angles and even if you can defend yourself from all of them, grappling is an all-to-common occurrence in conflicts. Turning yourself to the side does little other than help to offer the absolute vulnerability of your back to the attacker. Yes, the centerline is full of spots you want to protect, but now you can see that these are not the only or even the greatest areas of concern. Your lungs, spine, kidneys, neck, and base of skull are all exposed at your back and all have an extremely limited defense once revealed to an opponent.

To best understand why the tactic of always facing yourself fully to an attack is necessary, simply square your shoulders to a focal point in front of you. While standing forward, move your hands and arms around to see how easy it is to cover the vulnerable areas of your face and torso, all the while realizing that the risks of an assault to your back is severely limited.

Next turn to the side and realize how completely exposed your spine is and how absolutely limited would be your ability to block an attack leveled upon it. Spinning to the side forces you to fall victim to the limited rear-rotation of your shoulders. None can deny that the ability to cover vulnerable areas behind you has been completely restricted.

The best way to escape a crisis, as well as to evade unnecessary injury, is to prevent your weaknesses from the attacker. Realize all of your liabilities and never forget that your back is one of the most susceptible areas to debilitating injury.

Shoulders Turned Away From Attacker

The attacker squares off with you.

Your wrist is captured while your shoulders are turned from the attacker.

Shoulders Squared To Attacker

The attacker squares off with you.

Your wrist is captured while your shoulders are squared to the attacker.

A strike to the spine is easily landed to the exposed area of the back due to the lack of ability to protect it.

A strike is avoided by the continued ability to utilize the free hand.

5. When attempting to evade a confrontation, avoid choosing a technique that will restrict your escape.

Out of the pan and into the fire. This is an old saying that lends itself so easily to surviving a crisis. During a conflict, it is a common occurrence for many paths for escape to exist. The problem may therefore be present that with so many options ahead, you are lost as to which is the best to pick.

Just as in rule #2, you must consider that any avenue you chose to secure your escape may turn out to be a dead end. The sad truth is that, even when a course of action seems foolproof, random happenings and unforeseen variables may crop up. As will be outlined throughout this guide, the best practice is to always allow for a secondary or fallback route to your evasion of harm should your primary means of escape fail. In other words, unless you have NO other possible recourse, never move toward a direction of escape that will cause certain doom should it fail.

Of course you will feel the need to get away from the crisis as fast as possible, but do not allow yourself to fall victim to haste and fear. Always keep in mind that the first and most apparent path of evasion may not be the best. Unforeseen disasters happen when you force yourself toward a cut-off area of a room only to find out that the door you hoped to get through is locked and you are now pinned into a corner. Instead, allow yourself to take a single moment to choose a path that will leave your options open should it fail. Never commit yourself to any course of action, foregoing all others. You must always permit yourself to abandon a course of action should it prove faulty. Remember, *how quickly* you get out doesn't matter, only that you make it out does. Consider the following sequence.

Hasty Exit Attempt

Attackers present themselves in an environment with multiple opportunities for escape.

The crisis presents itself.

A choice is made to proceed forward to a possibly restricted path of escape.

The attackers are pulled out of the way of the desired exit.

Without allowing for the possibility of failure, the desired path is found to be inaccessible due to a locked door.

Neglecting forethought or a continued alternate means for escape, catastrophic failure is imminent.

To consider what other course of action would have been better taken, let us first assume nothing about where we have come from. In this sequence, instead of driving ourselves further into a field of aggression, it would have been more prudent just to return through the door from which you came.

Assessing Your Immediate Area/Diamond Points

Diamond points are designated for usage in your direct and immediate area, or more commonly, the area within your own reach. Unlike with your extended surroundings, defense of up-close physical action calls for the immediate area surrounding your body to be simplified to only four directions: front, back, left, & right.

Solo Diamond Point Overview

As you can see, once connected these points form the shape of a diamond, hence the name. Granted, this layout is a very simplistic and a broad generalization of the near area surrounding you, but split second and easy consideration of your surroundings need to be just that. The finer points of precise angles and exact degrees are unnecessary and may lend one to over-thinking the situation.

Sometimes active avoidance of the confrontation is not the best method to secure your escape. If engaging the aggression is your best bet, a few steps/considerations must be made first.

Dual Diamond Point Overview

Just as the near area surrounding you can be identified by diamond points, so is the area surrounding your attacker. Now is the time to choose your course of action. That being said, it is now important to recognize two separate, but equal applications of movement that will be available to you, Stealing and Forcing.

Stealing and Forcing

The best way to display the finer aspects of diamond fighting is to identify the practice in two parts: stealing and forcing. These are the two easy ways of altering your movement within the diamond points and the differences are quite simple. **Stealing** diamond points includes all of those movements in which you change your own position around the adversary and **Forcing** diamond points encompasses all of those movements in which you aim to alter the direction and stance of your opponent.

For the purpose of fully understanding the possible necessity of utilizing diamond points, the following sequences, as well as throughout this book, will be performed with ordinary objects serving as assumed exterior physical restrictions. Though the items shown are always the same, they are meant to represent every possible object or external impediment that might be in your presence.

Stealing Sequence

Let us assume in the following situation that there exists just one viable area of escape (marked with an X). As you will see, only by manipulating our movement around the opponent's immediate diamond point area can we find the availability to proceed upon the most direct and proper course to safety.

Stealing Sequence Scenario

The attacker approaches you while physical restrictions remain directly present.

The aggression begins and a path of escape is chosen toward the attacker's "Diamond 2" position.

Once the attack is thrown, quickly move yourself around the strike and toward the desired position (your attacker's unrestricted diamond 2 position). This will leave the force of the aggression to be placed forward where you had previously been standing.

After you have moved on a path to free yourself from physical restrictions and away from the immediate direction of attack, you will be easily able to turn toward a continued course of escape.

Here we have freed ourselves into open space and further constrained our attacker by simply knowing the limitations of our environment and acting accordingly.

Forcing sequence

Using a similar restriction to the previous scenario, we now observe an equally effective manner in which to gain the advantage over an attacker. While the assumption of the single possible path of escape is still present, a pattern of movement presents itself without the necessity of moving ourselves from our present position. Instead, we will simply use the direction and momentum of the attacker's aggression against them.

Forcing Sequence Scenario

The attacker squares off with you while only one direction of escape (your own Diamond 4) exists.

The attacker's strike is thrown and you simply steer the momentum of the aggression toward your Diamond point 2, leaving the route to the most direct escape (Diamond point 4) free to move upon.

Leaving your leg out, the attacker's uncontrolled forward movement allows for an easy trip.

Once the attacker is guaranteed to be free of restricting your path, you may proceed, without interference, toward your escape.

Timing Beats, Reading, and Preemptive Movement

Every altercation begins with an approach. Regardless of speed, distance, or surroundings, the conflict itself cannot commence without its own specific set of movements and, stating this truth, it must be recognized that every action takes time. To best understand, let us consider each one of these movements as independent events, or beats. Stopping, starting, turning, all will take a moment to perform. By appreciating this absolute need, we can observe that once momentum is introduced to an attacker, it cannot be arrested and reversed in the exact same moment. This is yet another reason why we aim to redirect, rather than simply resist energy.

Consider an event as simple as brushing your teeth. To observe that you need only put toothpaste on the brush and then shove it into your mouth excludes many of the necessary actions. First you must locate the toothbrush and place it in your grip. Next, the same for the toothpaste. Now, before the toothpaste can be placed upon the brush, the lid must be removed from the tube... So on and so forth.

These types of scenarios are often overlooked movements and may indeed hold the key to nullifying an aggression. Each one of the above actions is a necessity to ensure the goal. You must take into account that if a single one of the individual movements is restricted, let's say forgetting to take the lid off of the toothpaste, the entirety of the sequence becomes jeopardized. Consider the following.

Preemptive Movement Sequence

To move forward, the opponent will need to first move his rear foot (the right). This action of moving forward by using the rear foot must be repeated until he reaches his desired destination.

Now with the right foot forward, we can see that the left foot must now move to continue the attacker forward to his goal. Once the sequence of this foot pattern is recognized, you can now see that, based off of distance alone, the movements (2 steps forward) required by the attacker to reach you.

Once the second step is taken, the attacker is close enough to attempt a strike, but moving yourself forward into the approaching attempt, you will begin to be able to restrict the aggression by ceasing further forward movement on the part of the attacker.

Knowing that the attacker's body still has forward momentum, it must balance itself. Now we can see that, having taken the final step with his left foot, the attacker must stabilize his movement by throwing the opposite hand (his right), which may be easily blocked once seen in advance.

Herein lies the point: With practice, it is entirely possible to predict the necessary movements of an attacker before they are performed. It therefore becomes possible to alter the accessibility of a necessary piece of the attacker's sequence, consequently threatening the structure of the entire aggression.

The practice of this method is not as difficult as it may appear to be. The concept of beats can be broken down to a very simple sequence. Try to see the engagement of an attacker with the following thoughts: How long will it take you to escape? Where will your assailant be at that point? Next, how many movements are needed to achieve your escape? Where will your attacker be with the same number of movements?

Following are several examples of reading movements and the preemptive actions necessary to nullify each attack.

Blocking and Skewing Patterns

Blocking and skewing are two simple methods for controlling the path of a would-be aggressor. As was stated previously, each attack has a required set of events that must pass before an assault takes place. By utilizing random, ordinary objects that might surround, you will find that you may be able to manipulate the necessary actions your assailant will need to perform in order to reach you, thus granting you an opportunity to preemptively plan your own path of escape.

Easy Path Blocking Sequence

The attacker presents himself while physical restrictions are present.

Knowing that the attacker must move forward to strike, you choose to move one of the physical restrictions in order to impede his movement.

Laying the object directly in his path, you have removed his ability to directly approach you.

Once free of the direct approach, you are free to find an acceptable path of escape.

Easy Path Skewing Sequence

Once again, the attacker presents himself while physical restrictions are present.

Knowing that the attacker must move forward to strike, you choose to move one of the physical restrictions in order to impede his movement.

This time you utilize the physical restrictions to partially impede, rather than completely restrict the attacker's movement.

The indirect path you have left open for the attacker still being the fastest route to you, the attacker will choose to continue his aggression through the opening you have left.

Knowing the attacker's necessary, and now extended, path to arrive upon you, you are easily able to avert immediate contact by moving in the opposite direction.

Efficiency of Movement and Bodily Management

With the previously mentioned "beats" in a crisis already being recognized, it is important to realize that, while haste is a bad thing, the moments you will have to lay your actions are limited at best. Therefore, it is important to make the smartest possible choices with the limited time we will have for each movement. Here is where we must talk about body efficiency.

During a crisis, your brain must act as the command center over the rest of your body. Your arms, legs, hands, and feet will play the part of the defensive forces. Consider that you could be attacked on all fronts and realize that to send all of your protection in one direction, the rest of your areas will be left vulnerable and exposed. Here lies the importance of good bodily management skills. Consider the two sequences below.

Bad Efficiency Sequence

The attacker squares off with you.

A kick is thrown and the upper body is used for blocking purposes.

Good Efficiency Sequence

The attacker squares off with you.

A kick is thrown and the lower body is used for blocking purposes.

Having removed the available blocking from the upper body, a second assault is unable to be avoided.	Having maintained the available blocking of the upper body, continued defense is available for additional attacks.

As you can see, both seem legitimate reactions to the initial attack, but once the entire sequence is set into motion, you can see that one is much better of a choice. Try to place yourself into the mindset that if one arm is employed to block a strike, it is imperative to trust that it will perform its purpose and therefore you may leave the other appendages to cover their own zones. This practice will not only best protect you, it may also present numerous opportunities to strike back unexpectedly upon your attacker.

Proactive and Partial Engagement

Often times, crises may be controlled before they come to full fruition. Even once engaged into a conflict, it does not in any way mean that action cannot be limited or even utilized in pursuit of safety. You may have the ability to take control of your environment while only partially engaging your attacker. A limited and restricted amount of physical contact may provide you with enough freedom to escape the situation. So, what is the proper blend of acceptance and refusal to the conflict? How much engagement is enough? The answer is to utilize only that contact which is sufficient enough to secure your freedom.

Remember that as psychology and physics control the fighters, so do they effect and control the fight. Consider any simple block. When the aggressor throws an attack at you, your mind is flooded with seemingly useful information. Where is the aggressor's balance centered? Where is your own? How fast is the attack moving? How much momentum is contained within the strike? Which blocks are viable? If no blocks are viable, what is the proper course of action? Can I simply throw them out of the way with my defense? How do I choose what to do next?

Each and every one of these questions are very valid points of concern, but never forget that only one item of information is needed for your goal to be achieved in full: Which course of action is going to give me the best chance to escape?

The easy truth is that it is best to consider your attacker like any obstacle that is in your way and whatever the threat they may pose, you need only to get them out of the way. Your choice needs only contain that movement or tactic which is going to achieve that end for you. Following are several examples of common techniques utilized to free yourself quickly from an unavoidable physical confrontation.

Running sweep

The attacker squares off with you restricting the escape behind him.

You move forward to take hold of the attacker.

Continuing to move your force forward, you quickly sweeping your nearest leg behind the attacker.

Pushing forward as you move toward escape, the attacker topples backward, unable to restrict your forward movement and momentum.

Without need to find an alternate area of escape, you have simply moved forward to your goal by overtaking the path restricted by the attacker.

Clutch release

The attacker squares off with you.

As the attacker throws a punch, take hold of his arm, allowing the force of the strike to continue forward.

Using the same momentum he has used to throw a punch, you start to force the attacker off balance by pulling straight back.

Spin the release of the attacker away from you. With nothing to restrict the force thrown forward, the attacker will have great difficulty stopping his movement.

Once the motion is set forth, you will find that not only have you diverted the force of the strike, but you have also succeeded in pulling yourself in a contrary direction to the attack and also toward a clear path of escape.

Spinning Rip

The attacker squares off with you.

The attacker throws a strike and grabbing the outside of the strike with your nearest hand, you now begin to pull the attacker off balance by spinning your core out of the way.

By further turning your body out of the way, you continue to lead the attacker off balance.

Once the desired level of control is set forth, you may release the opponent in the desired direction while you, never stopping your own forward/circular movement.

Spinning Strike

The attacker squares off with you.

Grabbing the outside of the strike with your opposite hand, you now begin to pull the attacker off balance by moving forward to his side while spinning your core out.

Once free of the direct line of attack, you may level your own attack upon the exposed area of your choosing.

Once the chosen assault is laid upon the attacker, you may continue to spin your movement forward and toward a path of escape.

Spinning Throw

The attacker squares off with you.

Using your opposite hand, grab upon outside of the attacker's forward wrist.

Begin to move forward, spinning your core out of the way as you start to pull the attacker to the spot you have recently vacated.

Placing control over the back of the attacker's neck, begin to rotate the attacker by manipulating the direction of pressure.

Once rotation is in motion, continue the defense by lowering the attacker to the ground.

Once the attacker is on the ground, you may move forward to your chosen path of escape.

Full Circle Redirection

The attacker squares off with you.

Once the attack is thrown, drive your opposite hand directly on the outside of the attack with your palm up. This will temporarily hold your elbow down, but is necessary to make certain that no part of the strike lands on your core.

Once the attacker's strike is fully controlled and while it is still moving forward, quickly rotate your palm down, freeing your elbow to rise up over any restriction.

While rotating your hips in a circular motion, place your wrist on the back of the attacker's neck to create an equal and opposite direction of force.

Manipulate your attacker with this circular motion until the desired position is achieved.

Once you have removed the attacker's immediate threat, move forward to the safe escape path of your choice.

Simplicity of Engagement

Sometimes, even when preventative measures are laid forth properly, attacks cannot be avoided. In these cases, it is important to remember that you are to engage the attack for only as long as it will take to secure your escape. Complex, elaborate movements and combinations will aid solely in helping your attacker attach you to the scene. Proactive defense measures should be simple, effective, and have the ability to be performed quickly and repeatedly without adding to the time you are detained. Also, it is important to recognize that all of the following movements have the ability to be performed both in a preemptive situation (those to be executed before the actual engagement of physical harm is present, but still once you are absolutely certain that imminent physical danger exists) and in a reactionary defense (having the ability to be carried out as a response to an already commenced attack.) Consider the following:

Quick Eye Attack Sequence

The attacker squares off with you.

A quick strike is thrown at the eye of the attacker.

Sudden shock and a burst of unexpected pain overcome the attacker.

The attacker is temporarily subdued sufficiently for a quick escape.

Quick Throat Attack Sequence

The attacker squares off with you.

A quick strike is thrown at the throat of the attacker.

Sudden shock and a burst of unexpected pain overcome the attacker.

The attacker is temporarily subdued sufficiently for a quick escape.

Quick Heart Attack Sequence

The attacker squares off with you.

A quick strike is thrown at the heart of the attacker.

Sudden shock and a burst of unexpected pain overcome the attacker.

The attacker is temporarily subdued sufficiently for a quick escape.

Quick Genital Attack Sequence

The attacker squares off with you.

A quick strike is thrown at the genitals of the attacker.

Sudden shock and a burst of unexpected pain overcome the attacker.

The attacker is temporarily subdued sufficiently for a quick escape.

Quick Knee Attack Sequence

The attacker squares off with you.

A quick strike is thrown at the knee of the attacker.

Sudden shock and a burst of unexpected pain overcome the attacker.

The attacker is temporarily subdued sufficiently for a quick escape.

Chapter Summary

Regardless if the attack is pending or has actually begun, try to realize that it's not a bad thing to just keep moving as long as you make certain that your movement does not trap you into any restricted area. Feel free to delay and reassess the situation until a clear path of action is discovered.

Just as well and if needs demand, engage your attacker, but once you have manipulated your assailant to the point in which you may escape, do so immediately. There is no point or logic in staying behind. Your only goal is to secure your own safety. If there is even a slight chance that you are still in danger, it is imperative that you continue your escape.

Chapter 4

Multiple Attacker Strategy

Multiple opponents may be dealt with in much the same way as single attacker manipulation. Remember that regardless of how numerous your opposition may be, your chief aim does not change; get out of the crisis. There is no denying that the strategy of defending yourself against multiple attackers is more complex, but it does not need to be more difficult. Even the best fighters in the world cannot prepare for the possibility of every attack. This being said, it is best to remember not to resolve yourself to a course of action before movement has commenced. Only the existing circumstances may dictate your action. Following is a method in which you may best prepare yourself and assess your situation in a single moment.

Looking Like a Rabbit

There has been a long running joke among those who practice survivalist forms of kung fu that the advanced fighters always "look like rabbits" in crisis situations. This is not at all to say that they appear frightened in any way, but rather that, just like rabbits, they have taken the range and scope of their peripheral vision and placed it to its best possible usage to protect themselves.

Consider the restricted range of your forward facing vision. At best you may witness 180 degrees, or from one ear to the other. It cannot be denied that this limitation restricts your knowledge to only those attackers who might stand facing you from front or near sides and as anyone might guess, assailants do not limit their presence only to those areas in which you might best see them. Unfortunately, in trying to simply turn your head about, you will be removing the known attacker from your immediate view and possibly allowing him an opening for attack.

Next, place your view downward toward the area just in front of your toes. As you can now see, the range of your vision covers a much broader scope and can now better educate you to the presence of other possible assailants without removing the known assailant from your sight.

Restricted/Forward Peripheral View

Extended/Lowered Peripheral View

While this is an imperative practice to utilize when there are known to be multiple assailants, in truth, this technique should always be used, if only that you might rule out the unknown.

The Foolish Risk of "Conquering the Attack"

Grappling is arguably one of the best and most popular styles of fighting in the world. The techniques can be quick, effective, and thorough, but regardless of all of the assets of such an amazing practice, severe drawbacks must also be recognized in crisis management. By fully engaging your opponent with such methods, you not only allow yourself to be restricted and constrained to the scene of the attack, but you risk allowing yourself tied to one attacker, leaving yourself vulnerable to any and all additional assailants. Consider the following likely sequence.

Crisis Situation with Attempted Grappling Resolution

The attackers surround their intended victim.

Once the first attack is thrown, the intended victim moves toward the assailant to control the strike.

Taking control of the initial assailant, the intended victim chooses to attempt to control the attack by grappling.

With hands completely occupied with the first assailant, the second has no difficulty landing a devastating strike onto the spine.

With nothing to restrict the continuous attacks, assailant number three easily adds himself to the assault.

As the previous sequence showed, tying yourself up with full grappling disallows for the best chances of safety and removes the concept of elusion. Remember, your goal is not to win, it is to escape. However, this being said, it is not at all imprudent to utilize partial grappling engagements to such an end.

Utilizing Human Barrier by Means of Partial Grappling Engagement

You are approached by two attackers.

Having used your near hand to block the first strike, you find that you are now partially exposed to the second attacker.

Grasp on the hand of the first attacker and after having properly positioned your hands, you are able to rotate your opponent inward and yourself outward in the same motion.

Maintain the throw until your desired positioning of the attack is achieved.

Once the attack is controlled sufficiently, you may exit toward your chosen path of escape.

Making 2 Attackers Into 1

Fighting more than one person at a time is not only terribly difficult, it is unnecessary and ill-advised. The chances of escape and survival drop dramatically with every additional assailant who will confront you, but the elevated level of risk does not always need to be accepted. Several tactics (outlined in this section) exist to ensure that, regardless of how many attackers are present, you need only engage one at a time. The following techniques will provide you with the easy strategy you will need to properly position yourself and your attackers so that you may best prepare yourself for escape.

Single Line Creation

You are approached by two attackers.

Observing that a strike is about to be thrown, attempt to move yourself to the side of the attack furthest from the remaining attacker.

Use the force of the strike to propel the attacker inward while rotating yourself outward.

Once outside of the immediate attack, you will notice that the second attacker is unable to lay an assault upon you due to the presence of the first attacker.

Now, having controlled the possibility of further attacks, begin to position yourself toward escape.

Once choosing a path of escape, press yourself off of the attacker.

In having pushed the attackers into each other, you have as well projected yourself in the opposite direction and therefore on a path of safe escape.

Escaping More Than 2

Now let's talk about real trouble and the true essence of Survivalist Kung Fu. Situations exist in which multiple attackers may assail themselves upon you. Whether all attack at once or some choose to lie in waiting while others attack, your choice of action is all the more clear: Get out alive.

Just as with two attackers present, your objective is to limit, to the best of your ability, the number of opponents who are directly upon you. This practice may seem difficult at first, but as the following tactics will reveal, the performance of this objective may reveal itself to be easier than you may have thought. This being said, it is important to recognize the different types of multiple attacker assemblages, those who would encompass you within their numbers those who attack by all standing front. For easiest comprehension, the attackers will be listed as follows.

Multiple Attacker Overview

The Hostage Shield

You are approached by multiple attackers.

Choosing a path to the outside, you take hold of one of attacker #3.

Quickly position yourself to the outside of the grouping by swinging around behind the seized assailant.

Pulling back, begin to line your opponents up, guarding yourself with the assailant you have taken control of.

Once you have attained the position of your choosing, throw the restrained attacker toward his collaborators.

As the group moves into each other, turn yourself quickly and make for your escape.

As you can see, by repeatedly using the same tactics outlined for two attackers, you may easily use the presence of the additional assailants against each other. This practice may confuse if not entirely control the combined offense. Remember to keep the moves simple. Engage each attacker for only as long as needed and realize that you may need to repeat the same techniques over and over before your preferred positioning may be secured. Another method commonly used to overcome multiple attackers is called "braiding".

The concept with this next type of manipulation is that, with multiple attackers numbering greater than two, it is important first to make certain that no one is allowed directly at your back. Regardless of their positioning around you, you should be able to shift your stance enough to make sure that no one is straight behind, and thus totally within a blind spot. When you find yourself fully encircled by numerous assailants, the goal is very simply get outside of the circle.

Sequence 1 – First attack by Attacker #1

You find yourself surrounded by three attackers.

Attacker # 1 makes the first aggression. First, you quickly move to the outside of the attack itself and begin to spin yourself to the outside of the circle as well.

Next, temporarily restrict the movement of the remaining attackers by swinging the momentum of the strike inward and past attacker #3 and then into attacker #2.

Now, with both attackers #1 & #2 thrown into each other, you are now free to concentrate on #3 who is the only free attacker.

With the other two temporarily subdued, you may simply pull the remaining attacker's attempt at you out of the way, creating a pocket of escape.

Now free of restriction, your escape can be made.

Sequence 2 – First attack by Attacker #3

You find yourself surrounded by three attackers.

Attacker #3 makes the first move. Quickly move to the outside of the attack and begin to spin yourself to the outside of the circle.

Next, temporarily restrict the movement of the remaining attackers by swinging the momentum of the strike inward and past attacker #1 and then into attacker #2.

Now, with both attackers #2 & #3 thrown into each other, you are now free to concentrate on #1 who is the only free attacker.

With the other two temporarily subdued, you may simply pull the remaining attacker's attempt at you out of the way, creating a pocket of escape.

Now free of restriction, your escape can be made.

Sequence 3 – First Attack by Attacker #2

You find yourself surrounded by three attackers.

Attacker #2 makes the first aggression. First, you quickly move to the outside of the attack itself and begin to spin yourself to the outside of the circle as well.

Next, temporarily restrict the movement of the remaining attackers by swinging the momentum of the strike inward and past attacker #3 and then into attacker #1.

Now, with both attackers #2 & #1 thrown into each other, you are now free to concentrate on #3 who is the only free attacker.

With the other two temporarily subdued, you may simply pull the remaining attacker's attempt at you out of the way, creating a pocket of escape.

Now free of restriction, your escape can be made.

As you can see, by pulling the initial attacker inward to block the path of both remaining attackers, you grant yourself a very small, but very important moment you will need to prepare yourself for the next attack. Just as well, as you have witnessed, regardless of which attacker generates the first aggression, the usage of the formulaic tactic will grant you a viable means for escape.

Running Through the Wall

You are approached by a group of attackers, all who stand at your front.

As attacker #1 throws the punch, quickly move to the outside of the strike.

Knowing that the remaining assailants will now be encroaching, you control the strike and begin to position yourself.

Using the attacker #1 as a shield against attacker #3, you may now concentrate on the attack of the final remaining assailant, attacker #2.

By simply pulling the punch of attacker #2 out of the way, you have created a pocket to escape.

Knowing that the momentum of their strikes will force the attackers to continue moving forward, you are now free to find your escape.

As you can see, this is very similar tactic to the one outlined in the braiding sequences. In fact, most tactics for multiple attackers will use the same components. This is one of the many reasons that you should never bother to plan moves in an attack. By simple training (outlined in chapter 8) your body will simply be able to remember how to use the aggressions placed upon you to block future encroaching attacks.

Chapter Summary

Multiple attackers are to be seen as nothing more than an extra problem to be dealt with. Take your time and remember that if you are stuck, you may do something as simple as hold onto one attacker, blocking the other, until an opportunity presents itself to you. Make your move whenever you are ready, but understand at all times that every assailant must be checked before a safe escape can be attempted. Otherwise, your plans may end more quickly than you had hoped. After you have properly manipulated the variable of multiple attackers, you may then, and only then, proceed to the outlined tactics of escape.

Chapter 5

Weapons and Other Variables

The inclusion of a weapon or any other foreign object into a confrontation does not necessarily cause it to be a "game-changer" in and of itself; rather the implement should be seen more of as a "game-modifier." While its inclusion may intensify the crisis, it does not sway us from the main concern. The first priority never changes from escape, but now in tandem to that concern there must exist a second condition for your consideration. Therefore, to best prepare ourselves for the possibility of their inclusion, we must first understand exactly what are the individual properties of the instruments themselves and what can be the most likely intent of their addition into the attack.

Most Common Weapons

There are the six basic types of instruments commonly used in attacks. Each of the following share the collective components of having the ability to be used by anyone, are easily accessible, and need no special training to operate. It should also be noted that this list is not intended to be a comprehensive catalog of all of weapons in existence, but rather to include only those implements that are statistically the most regularly used during assaults.

1. **Edged Weapons and Piercing Instruments**: These tools are utilized for weakening the victim by means of stabbing or causing grave harm by incision. Though normally used for repetitious attacks, a single, well-placed advance may be grave enough to fully subdue the victim.

2. **Blunt, Striking Weapons**: Whether stick, bat, bludgeon, etc., these types of weapons are employed to induce concussive physical trauma upon potential victims, thus rendering them unconscious or so bodily harmed that they are unable to flee or defend themselves.

3. **Chains, Ropes, and other Loose Whipping Implements**: These "soft" seemingly non-lethal weapons are often considered less treacherous than others, but a single moment considering the possibility of asphyxiation will instantly dismiss that thought. Even sidelining the risk of possible death, they maintain the ability to quickly spread numerous points of attack over a great area upon the victim, causing an unusual amount of shock

and pain. Whether the fashion of assault is percussive, choking, binding, or even some-times cutting, these instruments can induce an incredible level of physical threat.

4. **Chemical Agents:** This refers to any projectile liquid or powder that can be propelled at someone such as mace or pepper spray. The aim of these agents is to impair vision and/or respiratory functions, or to impart harm upon the nervous system until the remainder of the victim's defenses are more easily conquered.

5. **Stun guns & Tasers:** These refer to any type of electro-shock weapon that may be used to temporarily disable the defenses of a victim. The effects, while only lasting momen-tarily, are extremely effective at rendering all of a person's defenses completely inoperative.

6. **Firearms:** Unfortunately the only probable malicious intent for these weapons to con-vey is death or severe bodily harm leading to death.

The above individual distinctions being listed, now we must recognize that while different properties exist and are respected for each weapon, it is the similarities between them that are overwhelming. Once each tool is seen merely as an extension of the attacker, it will as well be revealed to be restricted by the same overriding limitations.

As will be outlined in the following photo sequences, the specific properties of most weapons are irrelevant to a single, dominant, and shared constraint, distance. In fact, most weapons have an ideal range or "sweet spot" during an assault. It is important to realize that by restricting ourselves from this specific area, we might severely curb the damage that any weapon may produce. Consider some of these most commonly used weapons during an attack and their individual advantages and shortcomings.

Sticks and chains are rendered all but ineffective once you are removed from their im-mediate range. Tasers and Sprays have an average range of 15-40 feet, but require a direct line of attack. A simple step to the side may render the weapon all but moot. That being said, it does not matter whether we find ourselves too near or too far from their target area. Remember that once we are anywhere outside of range, the hazard of most instru-ments is extremely low. It is as well true that once inside the preferred range, or past the "Zero Point" of a weapon, it's effects will be vastly limited. It is true that bladed or projectile weapons will still remain dangerous (although their effects will be severely re-stricted) once inside the preferred range, but these are as well useless if you can keep your proximity sufficiently displaced. Consider the two following outlines.

Baton Past Zero Point

Knife Past Zero Point

The attacker presents a weapon.

The attacker aggressively moves the weapon toward the intended victim.

Choosing to drive into the attack instead of retreat from it, the intended victim simply moves forward and to the side of the weapon's direct path, thus past the point of immediate danger or "zero point".

The previous outlines will prove to be true for a litany of weapons, however, not to exclude the most obvious of feared weapons, let us discuss the tactics of survivalism once a firearm is introduced into the crisis. There is a single technique utilized here and it is one of the most common and easy of all movements you could perform. The answer is only this: run.

It is true that there are persons who are well enough trained that they might rush forward and control the absolute threat of this weapon, but even these highly skilled individuals will tell you that statistically it is safer to simply get yourself as far from this threat as fast you can. Hitting a stationary target from a distance can prove difficult for even an experienced marksman, but for anyone to readily and accurately hit a moving target, i.e. yourself fleeing from a crisis, will be even more difficult of a task. Don't make the attack easier for your assailant by staying close. It is true that the previous techniques can and do work upon an attacker wielding a gun, but they should only be attempted as an absolute last choice. The risk you take to execute these tactics highly outweighs the advantages there might be in such an endeavor.

Being Your Own Worst Enemy

No matter how bad a crisis is, you yourself can make it worse. How? By introducing a weapon into a situation. Regardless of your confidence and/or training with any particular weapon, you need to realize that the usage of NO weapon on earth is foolproof. Say hypothetically that you can actually prepare the instrument of your choice before your attackers are upon you. Let us consider the critical errors you have already made.

1. You have allowed yourself to become a participant of the conflict instead of trying to leave the scene.

2. You have foolishly assumed that the weapon will work without fail. All weapons can miss their target, adrenaline and shock can delay the onset of pain in an attacker, and even when tasers and sprays hit their mark, they can turn out to be positively ineffective.

3. You have tolerated the thought that using an instrument is worth the risk of it being taken away and used against you.

Ask yourself these questions... Can this weapon best every other implement known to man? Are you the single most talented person in the world with this particular weapon? Is it an absolute impossibility that this weapon be taken away from you and used against you? If you can answer no to any of these questions (and you know that you can) then you now understand why introducing any weapon into a crisis situation is a bad idea. Remember once again that you are not trying to conquer the situation, but escape it.

Projectile Knives and Other Thrown Objects

So you have decided to run. What if the weapon is thrown after you? It cannot be denied that one of the risks from any weapon is that it might be hurled in your direction, but this is not the absolute and imminent risk that it seems. Honestly, the most concern that you should carry over an object heaved in your direction is not that of an edged weapon, but rather that of a blunt striking instrument. The percussive damage that can be inflicted upon your body, even from a distance, might be great indeed. However, remember that even if a weapon is projected in your direction, you need only avoid contact once before it becomes a lost item.

Regardless, let us still discuss the finer points and concern of knives. Much unlike Hollywood has taught us, the actual level of hazard of having a perfectly placed instrument lodged precisely into a vital area is very low. Consider the following several reasons to best understand the lack of risk from a thrown knife or any other projectile such as a dart or throwing star.

a) **Special training needed:** To accurately propel a knife into a solid object takes practice, a lot of practice. Also, it should be mentioned that there is a quite limited range of damage these weapons may incur upon the body. It is true that random, unforeseen occurrences happen in the events of a crisis, but to assume that an amateur could not only have the proper knife to throw, but that they could also lodge it perfectly into a critical section of your body is bordering on fantastical. Needless to say, the same may be true concerning stars, darts, or any other projectile object. Also, unless it's a crime of passion from a known attacker, very few persons would allow the possibility of missing their target and losing the weapon only to have the authorities later find it with incriminating fingerprints on it.

b) **Special knife needed:** First of all, as far as knives go, most cannot be accurately thrown. Special knives, designed specifically for such a purpose, are necessary. Standard kitchen, lock-blade, switchblade and almost every other style of knife are bottom heavy and will be lopsided during rotation, therefore failing in an accurate attack. Secondly, the difference between throwing knives and tactical fighting knives can be gigantic. Throwing knives are predominantly a double bladed, piercing, not cutting instrument. True combat knives are designed for inflicting a series of small, very damaging cuts and penetrations into and along the vital areas of the body, not for throwing. It should be mentioned that combinations of the two do exist, but anyone with the knowledge to acquire such a weapon is hardly likely to risk losing it by throwing it away.

c) **Risk of a lethal shot is nearly non-existent:** Unless you are planning to crawl away from the attack, the chances of a deadly shot are miniscule at best. Why? The simple reason is this, the vast majority of knife-throw training is performed with the blade held and projected vertically. How can this matter?

Let us forget for a moment the overwhelming truth that knives are almost always rotated when properly thrown and this SEVERELY limits the attack to specific distances. In fact, it is this very vertical rotation that gives the weapon its penetrating force. However, even if a knife's blade were to hit you, your ribcage does not run parallel with the path of the flat cutting edge. Should the knife be propelled to enter into any of your vital organs in your chest, the small gaps between the horizontally running ribs will not be ample enough room for the blade to fit. This is not to say that no severe damage might occur from such a strike, nor to suggest that these are the only spots that a thrown implement can hit. Eye sockets, throat, and various arteries are among other, less structurally protected areas of your body. Regardless, it should be noted that while striking these other locations is a possibility, so is winning the lottery. The meaning: It's not that it would be impossible, but rather improbable.

With all of these reasons listed, it is best sticking to one fact: Your time would be better spent worrying about things that are much more likely to happen.

Too Close for Comfort

Sometimes a weapon is introduced into a crisis and before you know it, you are required to face the attack. This is by no means reason to despair. There are several, proper methods in which you respond to the inclusion of the weapon while still positively reacting to the concept of escaping the attack. This being said, several concerns must be addressed before you choose your response.

First, it is absolutely essential that you never let the business end of a weapon point directly toward yourself. Consider that it is a regular occurrence to see experienced teachers using rubber guns and knives to educate their students. The real reason for this common practice is not only to support visualization, but also to best educate their students on the specific direction of threat from the weapon. Even when a training aid is not available, these same instructors will perform empty-hand movements while seemingly pointing with the hand that executes the move. Whether the instrument they are pretending to have is a knife, a gun, or a canister of mace, the intended path and aim of the attack is realized. Remember that while it is perfectly acceptable to allow the bearing of danger pass between you and your attacker, you must never allow the threat to be pointed back at you.

Secondly, remember the concepts of bodily efficiency. Do not waste a single second or opportunity when defending yourself. Should you lose control of the weapon during a struggle and flight from the scene is not yet an option, use the nearest available appendage to the threat to regain control.

Next, if a random opportunity for disarming of your attacker happens, great, but don't center yourself on the idea. If you were trying to defeat the assailant, this would be a necessary tactic, but this is not your goal. The only acceptable response to a loosely freed or dropped weapon is to simply step on it, thus restricting its usage from the scene of crisis. Do not forget that your only job is to avoid the peril that the weapon presents.

Lastly, if you get lucky and the weapon somehow comes under your control, don't use it, throw it away. Why? Consider that people who bring weapons to a situation tend to choose a tool they are very comfortable with, offensively and defensively. Your advantage and maintenance of the instrument might be no more that a hiccup in their control. Try to think of every weapon as a beaker filled with acid. It doesn't matter who has the most control of it during a struggle, simply having it present in a fight is enough risk to want to exclude it from consideration and that it is best to just level the playing field and remove any chance for your attacker's advantage. Your safety and chances to escape will greatly increase once a weapon is no longer the dominant threat in a crisis. Following are three sub-sections of weaponry tactics.

Leading Away to Escape

The ideal method of action when a weapon is produced in an altercation is to simply avoid the weapon, allow it to pass you, and disembark from the scene as soon as possible with as little interaction between yourself and the weapon as possible. Observe the following techniques.

Vertical Circle Redirection

The attacker approaches you with a knife.

Using the nearest available arm, in this case the mirror side hand, you deflect the knife from the inside of the attacker's wrist.

Utilizing the same energy with which the knife was initially thrust forward, you begin to redirect the force and rise it upward.

Once the blade is overhead, you begin to prepare your free hand.

Transferring the momentum to your free hand, you are able to begin to lead the attacker off balance.

Now off balance, you may lead the attacker's entire arm over to your side.

Leaving the attacker to fall behind, you may quickly find your exit in the opposite direction.

Full Circle Redirection

The attacker approaches you with a knife.

As the attacker lunges the knife forward, you quickly move to the side of the thrust, again using your mirror side hand as the nearest blocking appendage.

Begin circling the momentum of the attacker behind you.

Continuing the circle, you prepare to let go of the attacker's arm while still spinning yourself toward safety.

Leaving the attacker to fall behind, you may quickly find your exit in the opposite direction.

Brush-Past Redirection with Strike

The attacker approaches you with a knife.

As the attacker lunges the knife forward, you quickly move to the side of the thrust, this time using your cross hand as the nearest blocking appendage.

Use your free hand to continue the attacker's forward momentum, circling your cross hand now downward in preparation for a circular strike.

As the attacker begins to fall off balance, lay a forceful hammer-fist blow on the back of his head.

As he falls from the strike, you may find your exit in the opposite direction.

Weapon Control Tactics & Disarms

Next, what happens if the ability to escape by simply deflecting the course of the weapon is not a viable option? What if, instead of avoiding the instrument, you find that you have "caught the tiger by its tail"? The truth is that moving to control the advances of an attacker is a natural reaction, albeit one that we should strive not to perform. However, if things go wrong (and they often do) and you find yourself either needing to capture or already having captured a weapon-wielding hand, you need to know what to do. Though the basic tactics for all disarmament are identical, each of the following techniques will be demonstrated with a knife only because of its most common usage.

To properly disarm a weapon from an attacker's hand you will need to first rotate their wrist to the furthest point it can turn before it will break. This type of torsion is called "Natural Torque." How do you know that you have achieved this level of torsion? Once the surrounding joints begin to rotate, that is a sign that the attacker's wrist can offer no more free movement, or "play."

Once that action is performed, it will be time to remove the weapon from the attacker's grip. Having taken the attacker's wrist to the point of natural torque where all of the free rotation of the joint has been removed, press against the SIDE of the blade toward the thumb and fingertips. Observe the following combined segments for comprehensive illustration.

Disarming Finishes

This section must be handled first solely for the reason that the overriding goal of disarmament is to remove the weapon from the scene. As stated previously, once a weapon is introduced into the crisis, one should take whatever precautions possible to restrict its inclusion as much as possible. By ridding ourselves of the weapon, we will as well rid ourselves of the danger that surrounds it. Consider the following two preferred responses after a disarming technique is achieved.

Disarm to Step

An attacker approaches you with a knife.

Seize control of the knife-wielding arm as it is about to strike down on you.

Just like revving a motorcycle, rotate your grip on the captured wrist forward toward the ground and prepare your free hand to assist.

Once having taken the wrist to a point of natural torque, lay your open palm against the side of the now immobilized blade.

Once the blade is pressed toward the attacker's fingers, it will simply fall away from the grip.

Step on the knife once it has landed on the ground to make certain that its usage is removed from the crisis as much as possible.

Once the knife has been removed as the immediate threat, you may continue to defend yourself accordingly.

Disarm to Throw Away

An attacker approaches you with a knife.

As the attacker advances, move yourself to the side and out of the direct path of the weapon. At the same time, take control over the outside of his arm with your mirror side hand.

Spin the wrist of the attacker forward and down, making certain that tip of the blade never faces toward any part of you.

Once the attacker's wrist has been rotated to the point where all free movement has ceased, use your open palm to press in the opposite direction against the side of the blade.

It is very common for the blade to simply not drop, but still become free to be taken effortlessly into your hand.

Once you have taken full control of the weapon, you may simply throw it away from the scene.

Active Disarmaments

Now that the two ideal endings of stepping and throwing have been identified and outlined, we will continue by addressing variations the disarmament of the weapon. It must be remembered though that performing either one of these final responses should result in your control over the weapon. Once under your control, your own usage of the instrument, as previously stated, should be restricted.

Forward Knife Assault with Rush-In

An attacker approaches you with a knife.

Once the knife is thrust forward, quickly swing yourself to the inside of the attack and inside of the attacker's guard. The best performance of this technique is to immediately block the blade hand with your wrist and cup the attacker's elbow with your free hand.

By quickly seizing and collapsing your forearm upon the wrist of the knife-wielding arm, you will have restricted the blade to a point well past where it could do you the most harm.

Now, turning your hips and pressing the side of the blade against your biceps, you will find that the knife simply falls into your free hand.

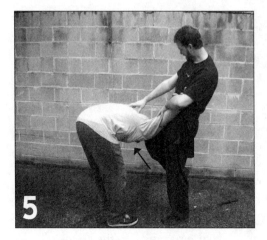

Now, once free to act, you may rise your knee to the captured attacker's chest.

And finish with an elbow strike to the spine.

Forward Knife Assault with Upward Disarm

An attacker approaches you with a knife.

Using your cross arm, grab the outside of the attacker's wrist, redirecting the weapon's path.

Once captured, rotate your own wrist forward, toward your fingertips, thus spinning the arm of the attacker.

Once the attacker's wrist is fully torqued, open the palm of your free hand flat to the side of the blade.

With slight pressure upward, the blade will come free against the attacker's immobilized thumb.

Inverted Knife Assault with "Takeaway" Disarm

An attacker approaches you with a knife.

Quickly raise your cross arm upward to capture the knife-wielding wrist.

Rotating your own wrist forward, toward your fingertips, begin to rotate the arm of the attacker.

Once the attacker's wrist is fully torqued, open the palm of your free hand over the attacker's grasp of the handle.

With only slight pressure, and due to the immobilization of his wrist, the handle of the blade will be released free from his hand and into your grip.

Inverted Knife Assault with Cross-handed Fold Back

An attacker approaches you with a knife.

Using your mirror hand, quickly rise to grasp the knife-wielding arm.

Making sure to press the direction of the blade's tip away from you, swing your free arm around and over the assailant's elbow.

Now, with two separate points of pressure, you have created an easy lever of the arm. Force the blade back toward the opponent by pushing on his wrist and using the inside of your elbow to pull the arm.

To finish, grasp the inside of your own arm and wheel the blade downward as you roll the lever, placing the blade against the attacker's neck.

Inverted Knife Assault with Mirror-handed Fold Back

An attacker approaches you with a knife.

Using your mirror hand, quickly rise to grasp the knife-wielding arm.

Making sure to press the direction of the blade's tip away from you, swing your free arm around and overtop the assailant's elbow.

Once again, with two separate points of pressure, you have created an easy lever of the arm. Force the blade back toward the opponent by pushing on his wrist and using the inside of your elbow to pull the arm.

To finish, grasp the inside of your own arm and wheel the blade downward as you roll the lever, placing the blade against the attacker's neck.

Forward Knife Assault with Continuing Directional Movement

An attacker approaches you with a knife.

Quickly move to the side, away from the blade's path and place your cross hand upon the outside of the attacker's wrist.

Once captured, use your free arm to rise up underneath the attacker's arm, creating a lock upon his elbow.

Begin to spin your hips to the far side, pulling the wrist into you to create the lever.

Once the movement has commenced, remove the lock of the arm bar so that you can use your now free hand as a guide upon the back of the attacker's head.

Finish the technique by forcing the attacker into any available barrier.

Multiple Attacker Weapon Scenarios

The tactics involving multiple attackers when a weapon is involved are quite similar to the movements outlined when the instrument has not been introduced. The main idea is to keep yourself as far from the danger as possible, using whatever or whoever you can to separate you. The main differences you will see outlined below are that you must observe more "proactive" defense techniques to create these obstacles, forcing the additional attacker to assume the closest proximity to the weapon instead of yourself. Following you will see two comparable scenarios. As you will see, regardless of the positioning of either attacker, you will need to utilize a more forward and forceful approach to disconnecting yourself from the immediate threat.

Two Man Knife Scenario (Partial Engagement - Hostage Shield)

Two attackers approach you, while the attacker facing you brandishes a knife.

By preemptively grabbing onto him, quickly steal yourself to the far side of the unarmed attacker.

Swing yourself around and behind the unarmed attacker to remove yourself further from the weapon.

Seize on the attacker to gain control and begin to lead him backwards using the "hostage shield" technique.

As the armed assailant moves closer, forcefully release your captive attacker forward toward the weapon-wielding hand.

Once you are removed from the entrapment and are no longer in the direct path of the weapon, you may make for your safe escape.

Two Man Knife Scenario (Partial Engagement - Clutch Release)

Two attackers approach you, now the attacker to the side brandishing a knife.

By preemptively grabbing onto him, quickly steal yourself to the far side of the unarmed attacker.

Move yourself fully to the outside of the crisis area, utilizing both the previously outlined techniques of the clutch release and the single line creation.

Once you are no longer in the direct path of the weapon, you may make for your safe escape.

Other Variables

It is necessary to accept that there are thousands of scenarios that can play out during a crisis. Your training may be well rounded and quite accomplished, but random occurrences might still loom above you. Ask yourself what happens if you been wounded or incapacitated in some way. Would you still know what to do? Consider also that you might not be alone. What is the preferred tactic if you find that you are attacked while there is a child at your side?

Regardless of your physical limitations or whom you find yourself in the situation with, the applications designed in this book do not change. In fact, the favored techniques for reacting to a crisis with an injury are the very same if you were to find yourself attacked while coupled to a dependent. Let us observe that while they must be respected and protected in their own right, these random inclusions are to be dealt with *only* as new dimensions of the *same crisis.* Whatever the addition or restriction, the surrounding circumstances do not change. The only difference is that these new limitations must hold us to a higher level of immediate consideration. To assume that we would react to them in any other manner does not make sense. Consider the following example:

If you suffered a broken wrist in a burning building with a knife wielding attacker present, the fact that the attacker was present, with a knife in hand, or that your own wrist is broken would not in any way alter your primary objective. While you will be forced to appreciate the reality of a higher level of threat, your own weakness and limitations, and a new dimension of difficulty in securing to your wellbeing, the fact of the matter still remains the same; you must get out of the building. Therefore your reaction must be that you do not allow exterior circumstances to change you from your goal of safety and preservation. Consider the following outline.

Simple Injury Observance Outline

Two attackers approach you while you are afflicted with a personal injury.

The assailants move in and knowing that letting an attacker get to your weak side will grant them a greater level of control, you quickly move to the outside of the attack, making certain to protect the injured side from contact.

Forcing yourself to maintain a position of protection over your wounded side, furthest from the center of the conflict, you utilize one of the techniques already outlined within this book (here a clutch release) to create a simple line of your attackers.

Once your attackers have been temporarily subdued and your injury is protected, you may find a direct line of safe escape.

Chapter Summary

Few experts can safely maintain and utilize a weapon during an attack, so the simple answer is this: even if it's not a firearm, Run. It may sound simple and it may sound cowardly, but it is statistically the best way to stay alive and well. If you cannot, consider that if your own self-removal from the conflict is not an immediate possibility, the avoidance and/or ejection of the weapon needs to be.

Chapter 6

Resuming and Resetting: Recollecting yourself when things go wrong, not if.

Kung fu teaches you what to do **when** things go wrong, not **if**. Despite your best efforts, mistakes do happen and suffering a misstep when attempting to escape a conflict situation is not just a possibility, rather it is an almost common occurrence. These occasions do not need to spell disaster though. Regardless of past faults, it must be known that there are always good choices that can be made as long as certain observations are respected. In truth, with just a few steps, you may regain control of a badly-turned situation. Listed within this chapter are some common and very effective practices to return you from ruin to a point of tactical advantage.

Assessing Your Current State and Choosing Your Path

Okay, you've been physically constrained within the scene of attack. First things first, make certain you take a moment to reassess the situation, don't just start thrashing wildly if things start turning south. Remember that rash actions can lead to harsh results. Wasted movement is wasted energy, and regardless of the adrenaline pumping through your veins, you need to control every asset you have. Whatever your placement, allow your senses of sight and touch to provide you with the information you will need to properly assess your current state.

Next, realize that even if full separation is not an immediate availability, you may still be constructive with your actions. Try to identify exact areas of pain or restriction. Consider everything about the sensations that surround these locations as any one of them might give you insight about how to partially diffuse the attack. The idea here is first to make sure that you don't make things worse, second to possibly begin to release yourself.

After the specific trouble spots are located, you may choose the best strategy in which to act. Once you are able to begin to relieve the identifiable points of distress, you will also open up new avenues of movement and thus proceed at least one step closer to gaining your complete liberation.

Restricting the Immediate Attack

Unfortunately, there is not always a bevy of time in which we can consider the best possible way to relieve ourselves from the constraint we feel during an attack because it is teamed with a continuing assault. If you find that there is no way that you can assess your situation due to an ongoing attack, it is best to protect yourself until a free moment produces itself. You will need to be proactive, but very focused on a single agenda; protect yourself from the continuance of the assault. Only by doing this will you be able to obtain a sufficient amount of time in which you can reconsider your current state. Herein is where we will discuss methods in which you might prevent or, if nothing else, delay the onslaught of an assailment.

Try to regard the situation as being akin to a soccer match in which your team is down by three goals. It would be impossible to score three goals all at once so there is really no point in turning your mind to that end. Instead, you must only allow yourself to attempt to get one goal at a time.

The obvious answer from this analogy is exactly mirrored when considering a crisis. Your goal must first be to endeavor to protect your immediate wellbeing. Only after this is achieved can you turn toward further goals and a continued plan of escape. However, this does not mean that must wait for the attacker to cease all aggressions to advance yourself toward escape. Remember that you may also consider movements that include those actions in which you may proactively move toward your goal of liberation. There is no reason that you should not take every opportunity available to you, but always bear in mind that no matter how confident you are in a movement or how eager you are to attain your freedom, you must make certain that the technique you choose centers upon your immediate defense as its primary goal. Following are a series of extremely useful methods in which you might both protect your wellbeing and aid yourself in getting to the next step toward release.

Stopper Blocks

An attacker approaches you.

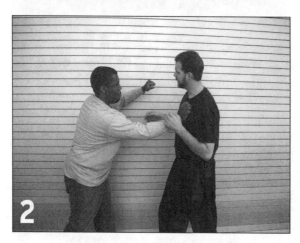

Before you can more properly react, the attacker takes hold of you and prepares to land a strike.

By aiming at the root of the assailment you can easily stop the assault. Also, with enough force applied to the block at this location on the attacker's body, you may cause a great amount of restricting damage to his muscle.

Reaction Strikes

An attacker approaches you.

Before you can more properly react, the attacker takes hold of you and prepares to land a strike.

To avoid the strike, quickly throw your arm forward, stealing the assault and blocking the attack with your elbow.

Return Strikes

An attacker approaches you.

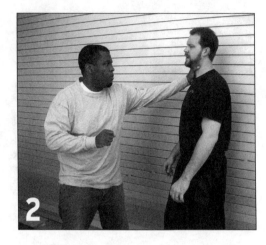

Before you can more properly react, the attacker takes hold of you and prepares to land a strike.

Catch the attacking hand with a simple block.

As the attacker moves to recoil and attempt again, use the backward pull of his arm as a window to your own open strike.

Quick Contact Separations

Once the assailant's attack has been suspended, it is time to use that momentary lapse in the assault to your best advantage. Consider though, before any drastic measures are taken, that your liberation might require no more than a combined effort of your bodily force in one direction. Consider the following examples of easy separation.

Press Off

The attacker has taken hold of you.

Press the entire force of your body against the attacker, using your hands as the contact points.

By pressing off, the force set forth should be more than enough to cause a separation.

Body Bump

The attacker has taken hold of you.

Ram the entire force of your body against the attacker, using your shoulder as the contact point.

By throwing the entire weight of your body upon the attacker, the force set forth should be more than enough to cause a separation.

Kick Off

The attacker has taken hold of you.

Raise your step to the press over the thigh of the attacker. Next, press the entire force of your body against the attacker, using the bottom of your foot as the contact point.

By kicking off against the attacker's leg, the force set forth should be more than enough to cause a separation.

Cannonball Head

The attacker has taken hold of you.

Ram the entire forward force of your body against the face of the attacker, using your head as the contact point.

The pain and force inflicted upon the attacker's face should be more than enough to cause a separation.

Quick Targets

If a simple, one-movement press off will not achieve the desired level of freedom, you may need to take a more forward approach to your liberation. In other words, you might have to level an attack of your own. Regardless of the areas open to you or the availability of your own specific appendages, you must strike. Following are several locations that may be sought during a crisis that will best produce effective results. Note that these spots have been listed because not only because they have been found to be the most effective areas of the body that have a good and regular availability during a crisis situation, but also because each has an open ability to be struck multiple times with multiple applications.

Eye Gouge

This strike is delivered forcefully into the ocular socket, aiming for a point of contact well past the actual eye itself.

Throat Strike

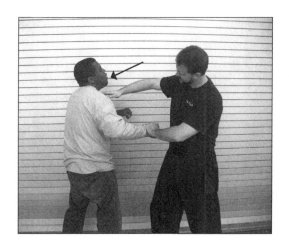

This strike is delivered with the joined fingertips and toward the air canal of the attacker. A correctly placed strike will interrupt the assailant's ability to breathe properly.

Heart Shot

This strike is delivered with either an open palm or a fully formed fist to the sternum of the attacker, causing severe pain and possible respiratory distress.

Knee

This strike is delivered forcefully upward upon either the kneecap itself or the shin area just below. A properly placed strike will cause extreme pain and severely limit the assailant's ability to physically harm or pursue you.

Genital Strike

This strike is delivered directly to the genitals of the attacker, thus causing extreme, movement-limiting pain.

It needs to be said after each of these that when trying to regain your freedom, you should remember not to allow a single failure to stop you. Whatever the reason, circumstances may emerge in which you cannot always be sure to produce an awe-inspiring amount of damage with a single shot. This may be true, but allow that with repeated attempts an adequate amount of damage might be inflicted upon an attacker to garner your release. Also consider that **ANY** part of your environment can be used as an asset. There are no rules when your life is at risk. Do whatever it takes to secure your safety and remember that if you do not achieve your objective right away... Try, try again.

Empty vs. Full Grabs

Up until this point, we have only discussed what are considered simple empty types of restriction, or grabs which themselves have no further agenda than to restrict movement. These versions of constraint may do little more damage than give you time to more properly assess the situation. However, now the time has come to consider those entrapment techniques that offer a bit more of a dilemma.

Let us consider that, even in the presence of an empty grab, there might be greater considerations than simply freeing ourselves. Case in point, multiple attackers. This situation may seem to be all the more reason to flee the scene in haste, but if we truly consider what is the risk behind the grab, we will realize that not only do these techniques grant us time to consider our options, but they can also prove to occupy the opponent(s) that are attacking us.

Consider that if an assailant focuses upon maintaining an empty grab, you may find the opportunity to lay your own assailment back upon him or even turn your attentions upon other attackers while his concentration is otherwise engaged. Observe the following scenario.

Proper Empty Grab Reaction and Defense

You find yourself approached by two attackers.

The attacker to your side seizes upon your arm with and empty grab.

Feeling that both of the entrapping hands offer no further danger, you allow the grab and focus your attention instead to grasping upon the approaching strike of the assailant at your front.

Controlling the strike, you raise your knee to level an attack on the assailant's midsection, all the while allowing the fruitless grab of his collaborator.

Once free of an impending attack, you may now turn attentions to releasing yourself from the initial entrapment.

Now, without an encroaching attack of his partner to concern yourself with, you begin to rid yourself from both the restraint and the attacker who placed it on you.

After breaking free from the hold, release yourself and begin to turn to a path to safe escape.

Once the best path of departure is found, take yourself quickly from the scene of crisis.

Okay now, what if the continuing attack does not include a strike? What if, instead, the restriction itself is causing harm or damage. *Full* grabs encompass all manner of grappling methods in which the constriction itself is the center of the attack. These types of techniques can number into the hundreds and may be set almost anywhere on your body. Consider that any joint might very well be placed into several different points of discomfort from numerous ways. Instead of listing every possible fashion in which you might fall victim to these techniques, it is more important to learn how to identify the path of your release.

> 1. Stop the pressure: Wherever the direction of force exists it is important to first arrest the strain. This can be achieved by either ceasing the pressure at its point of application or by moving your body around the grab, thus relieving the restriction remotely.

> 2. Locate the lever: Contradictory forces must exist for tension to exist. Identify the core spots of pressure, locate where the force is being applied to cause the stress, and prepare for the next step.

> 3. Choose method of alleviation: If the pressure cannot simply be removed from the point of the aggressor's inception, you must find an alternate manner in which you may maneuver yourself around the constraint to achieve relief.

For better illustration, consider the following two scenarios.

Lever Removal Release

An attacker approaches you.

Before you can more properly react, the assailant takes hold over your wrist.

Rotating your wrist forward, the attacker begins to gain control over your arm.

Your elbow, now exposed, allows the attacker's to form a perfect lever.

Pulling up by the wrist and pressing down at the shoulder, the attacker achieves a lock over your entire arm.

Recognizing the two points of contrary pressure, you begin to move your hand forward to relieve the pressure.

Choosing to make an attempt at the closest of the two points, take hold of the attacker's arm.

By simply pulling forward on the wrist, you will remove one of the contrary forces and thusly relieve the pressure.

Rollout Release

An attacker approaches you.

Before you can more properly react, the assailant takes hold over your wrist.

Rotating your wrist forward, the attacker begins to gain control over your arm.

You elbow, now exposed, allows the attacker's to form a perfect lever.

Pulling up by the wrist and pressing down at the shoulder, the attacker achieves a lock over your entire arm.

Pulling up by the wrist and pressing down at the shoulder, the attacker lowers you to your knee.

Continuing to press down, you find that you cannot in any way maintain your posture.

Unable to stop him, you find that you have been taken fully to the ground.

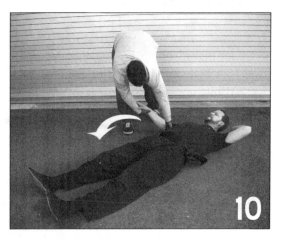

Knowing that you cannot stop the descent, you decide to use the force and rotation to begin a somersault and regain your control.

Once having completed the roll, you will find that the pressure on your arm has been all but released and also that now your attacker is wide open for a returned attack.

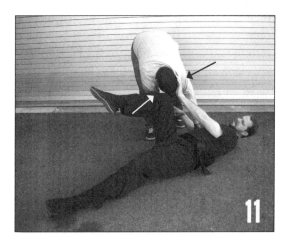

Using your free hand and a rising knee, you may deliver a devastating strike to the attacker's head.

Fully Upright Tactics

It may seem that you have failed if you find yourself constrained during an escape, but consider that if you are still upright, regardless of the confinement that has been placed over your body, you have maintained the most important of abilities; you are still on your feet. While upright, you can be certain to be able to take advantage of the first instance of freedom from your attacker. Following are highly effective releases from the most common methods of upright constraint.

Throat Release

When grabbed by the throat, it is essential to remember not to make a bad situation worse. How is this possible? In all honesty, it's easier than you would think. In an attempt to alleviate the constriction of a hand placed over your throat, most people would, by reaction alone, try to turn away from the hold. This is not a bad tactic... as long as you turn the correct way.

Spinning your body away in the direction of the attacker's fingers will prove to do little more than turn a throat grab into a rear-facing headlock. The reason why? The joints in the wrist can more than compensate for the rotation you will produce by spinning. To properly release yourself from the grab, you need only locate the direction of the attacker's thumb and turn your body in that direction. The limited range of movement in both the attacker's thumb and wrist will not allow the hold to be maintained. Observe the two variations.

Proper Throat Grab Release

An attacker approaches you.

Before a more proper reaction is laid, the attacker takes an intended victim by the throat.

The intended victim moves to cover the attacker's hand.

Improper Throat Grab Release

An attacker approaches you.

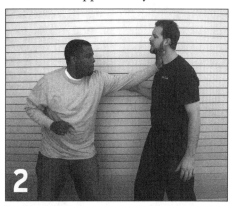

Before a more proper reaction is laid, the attacker takes and intended victim by the throat.

The intended victim moves to cover the attacker's hand.

The intended victim takes hold of the restraining hand, pressing the attacker's wrist down to his chest, and begins to turn in the direction of the attacker's thumb.

The intended victim takes hold of the restraining hand and begins to turn in the direction of the attacker's fingers.

By turning sufficiently and breaking the hold of the attacker's thumb, the intended victim has released himself from the restraining hold.

By turning toward the direction of the attacker's fingers, we find the restraining wrist maintains more than ample play to continue the hold.

Other Common Constriction Releases

Whether by the wrist, arm, neck, etc. an attacker may constrain you against your will. Normally, this would be a great source of panic, but with just a few considerations and proper practices, you will find that release is easier than you might have thought. Consider the following situations.

Punch Through

An attacker approaches you.

Before you can more properly react, the attacker takes control of the inside of your wrist.

Punch straight forward over the shoulder of the attacker.

Complete the release by raising your hand slightly at the very furthest extension and fully remove yourself from the hold.

Quick Change (Descending)

An attacker approaches you.

Before you can more properly react, the assailant begins to take hold over the inside of your ascended arm.

To begin the release, angle the fingers of your constrained wrist downward toward the arm of the attacker.

Finish by arcing your own wrist downward and stealing the grab from your attacker.

Quick Change (Rising)

An attacker approaches you.

Before you can more properly react, the assailant begins to take hold over the top of your lowered arm.

To begin the release, angle the fingers of your constrained wrist upward toward the arm of the attacker.

Finish by arcing your own wrist upward and stealing the grab from your attacker.

Assisted Grab Release to Eye Gouge

An attacker approaches you.

Before you can more properly react, the attacker takes hold over your wrist.

Choosing to utilize your other hand to achieve the release, place the palm of your free hand against the side of the wrist underneath the attacker's small finger.

Holding the palm of your free hand to serve as a barrier of free movement, swing the elbow of your captured arm inward, making sure not to attempt to bring the wrist with it.

Unable to maintain the hold, the attacker will have no choice but to allow your captured hand to go free. Once this liberation from entrapment is complete, use your liberated arm to strike a finger gouge forward into the assailant's eye.

Snake Up The Branch Wrist Grab

An attacker approaches you.

Before you can more properly react, the attacker takes control over the top of your wrist.

Use your hand to circle up to the outside of the attacker's wrist.

Continue the circle over the wrist until the assailant's hold is broken.

Snake Up The Branch Arm Grab

An attacker approaches you.

Before you can more properly react, the attacker takes control over your arm.

Use your whole arm to circle up to the outside of the attacker's wrist.

Continue the circle with your elbow over the attacker's wrist until the hold is broken.

Elbow Roll

An attacker approaches you.

Before you can more properly react, the assailant begins to take hold over the top of your wrist.

To begin the release, lift the elbow of your constrained arm up around the outside of the hold.

Once you have reached a point in elevation higher than the attacker's arm, hook the tip of your elbow over and begin to press down.

Continue to press down with the elbow and start to pull up by the wrist. This combination will succeed in making your arm into a lever, thus you will achieve full liberation from the hold.

Headlock

An attacker approaches you.

Before you can more properly react, the assailant begins to take hold over you.

Jumping in quickly once contact is made, the attacker places you in a forward facing headlock.

To being your escape, raise the arm nearest to your attacker upward from behind.

Throwing your arm down over in between your two heads, lay your hand against the attacker's chin.

Your liberation can be attained by pulling backward on the chin and standing to straighten your back.

Defense of Violent Projection into a Barrier

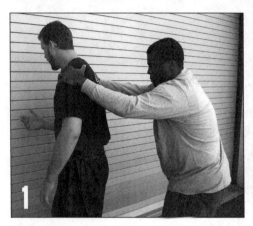

An attacker grabs you from behind and begins to force you, face first, into a hard barrier.

Quickly force the back of your hand directly in between your head and the wall.

As you are forced into the barrier, guide your head to fall against the soft, muscular tissue on the inside of your arm, thus protecting the most hazardous and at-risk region of your body.

Once the forward pressure has ceased, begin to brace yourself for a push-off with the bottom of your foot.

Maintain your balance by placing the opposite hand against the wall to assist.

Pressing as hard as you can with both arm and foot, force your entire weight to the rear.

Once you have removed yourself from the immediate contact with the wall, begin to spin yourself to the outside of the attacker's hold before he can simply reissue the assault.

Once removed from the direct line of pressure, begin to guide your attacker's force to allow him to fall forward past you.

Finally, by spinning your hips fully, utilize the resistant pressure of the attacker to make him collide into the wall in your place.

After an Untimely Descent

It is easy to panic if you find yourself unexpectedly taken down to the ground, but this is no time to lose your head. It may take a couple more steps to attain your freedom, but there are many quickly performed tactics that can set you right back on the path. First assess your level of restriction to the crisis; catching you balance with your hand is a lot different than being face down on the pavement. Once you understand your situation, try to identify the necessary steps it will take to right yourself to proper posture. Only after you garner that information will you be able to properly act. Consider the varying series of techniques within the following two categories.

Semi-descended tactics

It doesn't matter if you get knocked down onto one knee or both, things aren't as bad as they seem. The fact alone that you are still maintaining a semblance of posture is enough to assure you that your assailant has not taken complete control over you. When semi-descended, whatever your current position, you need to recognize the overriding goal necessary to return yourself to safety: get back up. This task is most easily achieved by locating the weakest point of your attacker's control. After this is accomplished, you may subsequently find your way back to standing fully upright. Remember that one knee down is enough to pin you to the site. Observe the following.

Descended Headlock

An attacker has placed your into a descended, forward-facing headlock.

To begin your escape, raise the arm nearest to your attacker upward from behind.

Throwing your arm down over in between your two heads, lay your hand against the attacker's chin.

Pull back on the attacker's head as you begin to straighten your back.

Your liberation can be attained by further pulling backward on the chin and standing.

Fully-descended tactics

Now it's time for a bit of controversy. What is the best tactic to utilize once you have accidentally fallen or after being taken fully to the ground against your will? The answer: Get on your back. Yes, many martial arts will tell you that placing your back against the floor does little more than keep you pinned to the ground and further restrained to the attacking environ, but in the world of survivalist kung fu the action of staying on your back will, if only temporarily, allow you to face your attacker and leave your hands, arms, feet, and legs ready for the immediate defense.

Yes, if the situation was different, it might be wise to stay on your stomach to better prepare yourself to get your feet under you so you might better able to flee the scene of attack. However, there will be no point in trying to escape if you cannot guard your spine, lungs, and the back of your head. Remember the lessons of chapter 3; It is imperative to maintain the active ability to employ hands and feet as both offensive and defensive weapons so you can best prepare yourself for the next step. It cannot be denied that by facing your opponent, you will have a much better range of attack, as well as a greater possibility of being able to utilize a myriad of low kicks to aid in defense. Remember that only once the attacker's threat is neutralized should you allow for the exposure of perilous and vulnerable areas.

To sum it all up, it is not that we forget in a crisis situation that our prime objective is to leave, but rather we understand that the risk of these previously listed injuries highly outweighs the need to instantly flee the scene of attack. Following are two sequential methods for escaping this common type of restriction. The first centers upon getting on your back. The second focuses on how to proceed once you are on your back. A.K.A. resisting the immediate attack and finding a way to safely leave the scene.

Switching the Mount

You find yourself pinned, face down, to the ground by an attacker.

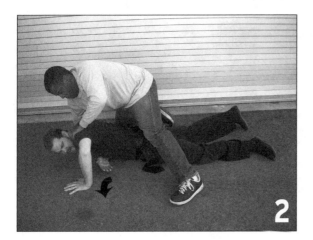

Slip your hand underneath your core.

Once your hand is beneath you, start to rotate your shoulders to face your opponent, mirroring this same movement with your hips, allowing both your hand and lower leg to begin to slip underneath.

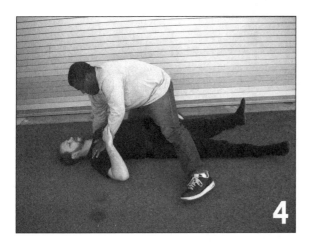

Continue to rollover until your position is face up.

Freeing from Submission and Safe Release

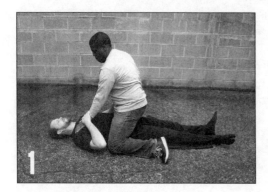

Whether by rolling yourself over from a face-down mounting or by simply falling to your attacker's pressure, you find that you are on your back with an assailant on top of you.

The attacker prepares to strike.

Raise your cross hand quickly up to the outside of your attacker's downward strike.

Guiding his hand downward without stopping the force of the strike, collide the attempted punch into the ground.

Once the strike is nullified, pull the attacker's manipulated wrist and begin to add a counter pressure to the elbow. This will begin to allow you to commence rolling yourself from underneath.

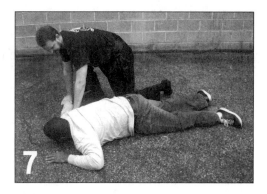

Utilizing the contrary pressures upon the opponent's arm, arrange an arm bar and press it fully against the ground.

Once the arm bar is complete, carefully raise one leg.

You may rise to a full standing position as long as you allow your weight to remain over the constrained arm. In other words, though it seems wrong, it's okay to bend at the waist to maintain the hold.

Once fully standing begin to guide yourself toward an exit, making sure to always continue the arm bar as you move.

Once assured of your safe exit, simply release the opponent and move quickly toward your exit.

Understanding Injury

Lastly in this section, and to be properly and honestly prepared, we must discuss a probability. It is a cruel reality that absolute safety cannot always be secured, however the need of "absolute" may be an unnecessary burden. Sad, but true, is the reality of needing to understand the difference between pain and injury. Furthermore, there must be a distinction between non-consequential injury and injury that causes impairment.

Why must these be recognized? Rare is the attack that can be exited from without a single scrape. Injuries can and do occur even for experts. However, regardless of the harm incurred during an assault, it is imperative to move forward toward your escape. Consider that if you can remove yourself from an attack of ten armed men trying to kill you and you suffer only a broken finger as a result, this must be viewed as a success. **This is not in any conceivable way advocating a willing sacrifice of any part of your body to an attack. Rather it is instead offered merely as a consideration of how to respond AFTER an injury has already been received.**

Chapter Summary

As was stated before, try to control your panic. Allowing panic to control your emotions during a temporary setback will prove only to extend the crisis. Cover yourself as best you can to protect from the attack and allow your thoughts to slow down so you can come up with a clear plan.

Remember that time will pass and so will the crisis. If no clear path is present, try to mentally remove yourself from the situation. You may be too close to realize what is best, but if you can allow yourself to step back and see the entirely of the scene, not just the present end, it may not seem so unconquerable.

Chapter 7

Prioritizing your Defense & Escaping the Crisis

As has been stated many times throughout this book, escape is the most important goal you should think of during a crisis. In the past, a regular tactic of self-defense training was to get your attacker on the ground during an assailment, however you could, and then lie down next to them and start kicking, shouting an audible demand: "No! No! No!" This has got to be the most nonsensical and ludicrous idea ever. As if the attacker didn't know what they were doing was wrong, or perhaps assuming that they didn't understand that you didn't like it. This notion could not be more foolish or dangerous.

To choose to stay within a conflict once you are free of an assailment in your immediate area is just being irrationally reckless. Remember that attackers want to restrict you to the scene of the crisis and this practice gives them exactly what they want. Never allow yourself to fall victim to this type of insanity. No matter the circumstances, just get out of the situation, however you can and do not concern yourself with telling the aggressor how unethical and inappropriate their actions were.

The point of this chapter is centered upon the wise decision of continuing your escape upon the event of your immediate area being clear and once you are left to concentrate upon the continued dilemma of escaping through the extended environ surrounding the attack. Following are a variety of common practices, relevant considerations, and effective tactics for removing yourself from the extended scene of a crisis.

Proactive Preemptive Movement

Just as was discussed earlier, the idea of knowing where your attacker is going to be before they get there is a remarkably valuable asset. However, in this chapter we are going to discuss a new type of preemptive consideration. The idea within this section is not only to identify the probable path of the assailant and temporarily restrict them from you, but rather to be able to continuously aid in the ability to alter their course to your liking, if not eventually block it complete.

Remember that by understanding the necessary route that your attacker must take, you will be able to utilize the surroundings of your environment to your advantage. Consider the following mixture of two sequences (blocking and skewing) discussed in Chapter 3. As you will see, if we consider each sequence merely as a single piece of a larger system, rather than independent techniques that must stand on their own, we may combine them like puzzle pieces that fit together in any order in which we need to utilize them.

Combined Skewing and Blocking Practice

The attacker presents himself while physical restrictions are present.

Again, knowing that the attacker must move forward to strike, you choose to move the physical restrictions in order to impede his movement.

To begin, you choose to utilize the physical restrictions to partially impede, rather than completely restrict the attacker's movement.

Once misdirected toward the direction of your choosing, you move next to further restrict contact.

Now laying a physical restriction on the most direct path to follow you, you have allowed for a greater chance of continued escape.

Multiple Attacker Environmental Tactics

You find yourself facing two opponents in an environmentally restricted area.

Utilizing your surroundings, you choose to limit the attack.

Throwing an obstacle in the path of one attacker, you are free to negotiate the attack of the other.

Making sure to maintain the obstacle between, you may begin to engage one of the attackers.

Continue by pulling the engaged attacker in the very same direction that you have misdirected the initial attacker.

Once their momentum and direction are controlled, you will find an avenue for escape.

By controlling the attackers and limiting the environment, you should have ample opportunity to find a ready ability to escape.

The Myriad of Emerging Considerations

It need not be confusing to decode and continue on your path once the onset of a physical conflict has begun. Let us assume that you have utilized the previously outlined tactics to protect yourself and your immediate safety has been preserved. What happens next? This is the essential question that should precede your every movement before, during, and after the conflict.

Just as was outlined as a rule in the previous section common mistakes not to make, the short moments needed to be spent in consideration for securing your safety are the same before or during a conflict.

Consider the old Chinese fable of the fisherman who saw gold coins at the bottom of a pond. Without forethought, the man jumped into the water after his prize only to realize that he didn't know how to swim. Your movement may be momentarily useful, but if you move upon an avenue of limited possibilities without consideration of repercussions and you may find yourself "at the bottom of a pond."

So how do you choose? How can you possibly make such an important decision in such a short amount of time? You must remember that while expediency is absolutely called for, haste is not. Remember that a mere second, well spent upon observation of your environment, will increase your chances tenfold over just running blindly from the attack. Survey your surroundings and allow your mind to be open to the fact that the most obvious path of escape may not be the best one. Only once you have decided on the best possible path for escape should you begin to attempt to position the attacker as well as yourself to achieve that goal. Herein is where we must remember ourselves to the immediate vs. extended areas.

Prioritizing and Recognizing your Line of Escape

To look at the first of the two pictures above may leave you wondering what would be the best course of action, but if you simply remove the immediacy of the attackers' impending threat (as done in the second picture) your necessary line of escape from the scene of crisis can be made absolutely clear. After this overriding need is discovered, you will best be able to plan your departure to safety.

Process of Elimination

Upon the realization of a crisis, observation of your surroundings is a must, but it is not always essential to come up with the perfect escape plan right away as this isn't always immediately possible. However, in place of an obvious escape, we must find another means of knowing where to go. This is the time it becomes necessary to recognize the NON-viable routes that surround you. By simple process of elimination we can rule out harmful paths of movement and then judge how it is best to proceed with what avenues are still open to us.

First, take a quick look around. Do you know the area you are in? Do you know a certain door is always locked or if it leads into a closed-off space? Whatever previous knowledge you have about your surroundings, that supersedes all other escape plans.

Also consider common knowledge, such as what story of a building you are on. To be trapped in a single story house, in a room with three locked doors and a single open window shows clearly how even with multiple "common" departure points from the scene, the alternative will be much better. However, what if the room you find yourself in is on the second floor or higher? The window may no longer be an option, but this does not necessarily spell certain doom. It only means that you need to keep looking. Yes, the doors may be closed and possibly locked, but what if one of the locks is on your side of the door? If needs be, could you break a door down (possible if the doors open away from you) If you can answer yes to any scenarios like these, then the path will not be listed as a non-viable route and you will have found your avenue of escape.

You can now see that you are just as dependant on knowing where you can't go as knowing where you can. Once you have removed all known non-viable routes of escape you will be left with the remaining possible options and then be left to make your best choice for escape.

Best Guess

Even if your surroundings are unknown to you it is still important to utilize the process of elimination to begin to secure your escape. Once these areas are eliminated it is necessary to choose the best possible method of escape. Following are some key assets and detriments to keep your eyes open for.

Indoor Attack

Hot spots to avoid:

- Doors that lead further in
- Locked windows
- Wall Corners

Doors that lead further into the structure are much more likely to be trap points. The entryways indoors tend to be restrooms, closets, and other enclosed areas that do not commonly regularly require a second exit or even window. Locked windows only inclusion might be to shatter upon you should you be forced into them and corners will leave you trapped in three directions while your attacker controls the remaining side.

Advantageous assets:

- Doors that lead to retraced entries
- French doors
- Windowed walls

If possible, retracing your path of entrance is obviously preferred for the reason that you already are certain of the path of escape. Unless your entry into an area was long and complex and a better means of escape is readily apparent, the retracing of your initial entrance may serve as the best possible means of escape. Like it has been said in many situations before, the devil you know is better than the devil you don't. As far as French doors are concerned, this refers to any door that has an easy lock to break past. This may sound drastic, but remember that your life is worth more than property. If you are absolutely certain that you are under a grave physical threat and a clear and ready means of escape can be made by breaking the weak lock on a French-door, know that the price you pay for the door will almost certainly be less that the hospital bill and fees for any physical therapy. Lastly, windowed walls on the ground floor are preferential solely for the reason that our initial entrapment is only one breach away from being overcome, but make certain that you can recognize the difference between natural and artificial light or you may be delving further into an entrapment.

Outdoor Attack

Hot spots to avoid:

- Blind alleys
- Choked avenues
- Closed-off urban areas

Each of these above listed hot spots is included for the same reason; the danger of leaving yourself trapped. Areas such as blind alleys, zero outlet streets, wall-enclosed parking lots, etc. all offer severe restrictions to the possibility of escape paths, not to mention granting our assailants the privacy needed to fulfill their attack to the furthest extent.

Advantageous assets:

- Open, populated areas
- Areas where you can create obstacles between you and your attacker
- Retraced entries

Open areas that are high in population are not preferred only because of the hope of a good Samaritan, rather what we seek to find here is more along the lines of witnesses. Sad to say, but this is statistically a greater deterrent than attackers fearing random persons coming to your rescue. Furthermore, these same open areas will provide a greater chance that we will be able to utilize and manipulate obstacles that can make it difficult for an assailant to pursue. Lastly, and once again, returning from where you came may prove to be the preferred and most secure means of escape.

Line of Escape

Once your area has been properly assessed, you will be left with whatever options still remain. This is where you will choose your line of escape. The line of escape is simply the path of least resistance to your safe departure of the scene. Consider the outline below.

Line of Escape

You are approached by two attackers in a closed-off space.

As the attackers begin to approach, you identify your best possible route to safety.

Move yourself slightly in the direction of your desired path, pulling upon the attacker who is most blocking the route.

Push the attacker into his cohort and use the force and motion of the pull to spin yourself away from the conflict.

Once free of the entrapment, you make a safe exit.

Lead Away

You are approached by two attackers in a closed off environment, both of which blocking the desired path of exit.

Feigning slightly to the side, lead the attackers to follow your movement.

Once they have commenced on pursuing you, quickly spin yourself out of the way.

Before they can mirror your movement, turn to the uninterrupted path to your freedom.

Make a safe exit once free of the entrapment.

Unconventional Escape Paths and Patterns

Situations arise where a conventional means of escape is just not feasible. Many times, commonly used paths of escape are blocked, locked, or restricted due to some other reason that makes them a non-viable route. This is where tactical training comes into play.

Alternative escape patterns utilize unorthodox means to secure an acceptable escape. The idea is to access safety through a method that your attacker(s) has not considered or restricted. This is not to say that quickly jumping through windows is a good thought. IT ISN"T. Unfortunately, Hollywood movies have allowed some of us to believe that the impossible is possible. Only if the window has been broken with another object and cleared completely from its frame should this EVER be considered a potential option. Otherwise, grave injury or even death may occur. Consider instead something as simple and realistic as running through hedgerows and people's gardens or jumping over a low banister.

Post Evasion Preservation and Continuance Steps

Unfortunately, simply being able to leave the site of an impending attack does not mean that you have secured your safety. Once you have achieved your exit from the scene of crisis, it is important that you do not allow yourself to simply rest easy. Theses is still more work to be done in order to ensure our wellbeing. Remember that all an attacker needs is their own legs to follow in pursuit and until you are **absolutely positive** of your safety, a grave threat may still exist.

Upon the cessation of immediate danger to your body, proceed quickly away from the scene, creating several angles in your path as you go. This method of escape is used in order to establish a visual disparity between you and your attacker, thus making it difficult for anyone to follow you. Though you may not be completely certain of the exact lay of the land, do your best to not just proceed randomly from the site of attack. You should always have a goal in mind: Try to get to a safe or populated area as fast as possible.

Following you will see a sequence of an attacker (X) in pursuit of an intended victim (O). The cone ahead of "X" represents the attacker's field of vision.

Escape sequence utilizing angles accompanied by overhead chart

 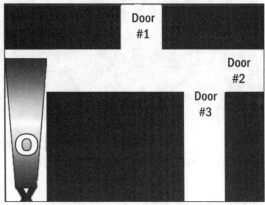

A crisis emerges in a closed-off space.

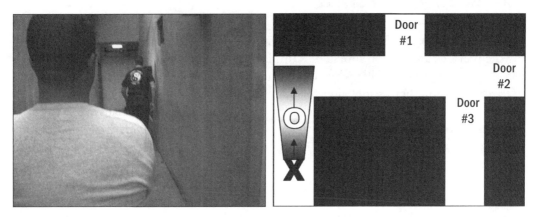

Pursuit begins.

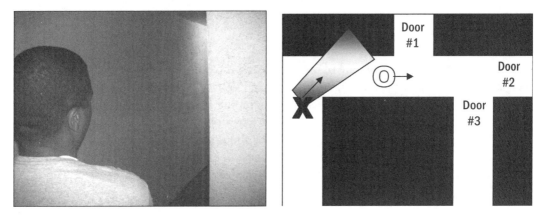

The attacker cannot keep visual contact with the intended victim.

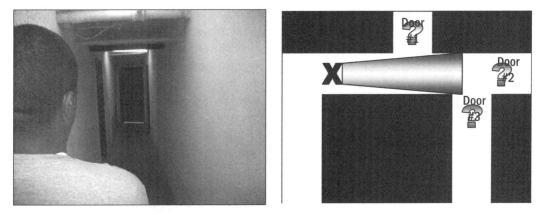

With many options available for the victim's escape, the attacker does not know which way to follow.

The Falsehood of Forfeit

Lastly, while the path you will choose might not be black and white, the choice of utilizing the previous application should be. This is not to say that your escape will not come without certain pitfalls, rather while these consequences should be respected and observed in their own right, they cannot alter the fact that your need is to immediately move on. The world and indeed the attack will not stop if you stub your toe. The answer to each peril is a simple one: Get out. This is the only thing that should occupy your thoughts during a crisis. You will have plenty of time to lick your wounds once you are safe.

Let us now observe two separate types of fruitless concerns. First we will consider the distress caused by an unexpected occurrence during the altercation. Consider the following questions. What if you are physically harmed before your escape can be secured? What if your injury is grave? What if you sustain a knife wound or worse? What if you need immediate medical attention? Even these extremes cannot change your agenda. If your liberation from danger cannot be secured, you have removed any chance that a doctor will see you in time.

Next are anxieties for the welfare of our future and the questions that will arise from that. What about the fear of retribution after the fact? What if your safety is secured and now you must consider future legal ramifications stemming from your escape? If you allow your mind to be clouded by future worries, you may not survive to face them. It is true that these concerns are extremely valid, but they should not enter into your mind in the stead of your own safety. I wish to be clear that no one can promise a positive outcome for these apprehensions, but this does not alter that each problem must be dealt with as it happens, not before.

Chapter Summary

It is important here to remember once again that your only job is to escape the conflict, but remember that this task does not need to be complicated. Your escape might be as simple as feigning one way to lead your attacker away from an exit. Regardless, once you are free, don't look back. Taking a quick glance is just the same as almost getting into a car accident and then pulling your eyes away from your path to watch the accident that you didn't get into. The risk of another accident hugely outweighs any desire you should have to see what happened.

It is senseless at this time to worry about what you have done to get to a point of liberation or how you did it. Getting out quickly and getting out alive are the only things to consider. Also, try to remember that until you are 100% sure of your absolute safety, you are still within the conflict, so keep running and try to locate continuing escape routes all the way.

Chapter 8

Practical Escape Training Drills and Preparation

It is a good thing to understand the instruction outlined throughout this book, but it is another thing altogether to prepare yourself to actually perform the necessary practice. It would be a rare thing indeed for someone to simply read the proper approach to strategy, never train on any of the subjects, and then perform the applications flawlessly upon the onset of a crisis. To realistically prepare yourself to overcome a crisis situation, you must learn to practice and train yourself in advance. Here is how to do both:

Mental and Pre-Training Preparation

It is absolutely imperative that you understand what you are doing before you do it. This sounds ridiculous, but all too many times, students jump into practicing moves they have seen without understanding what the techniques actually do, how they work, or when they are to be used. Certain rules must be observed by all participants before any physical phase of training is attempted. The following guidelines are present not only for their aspects of safety during training, but they are present to allow accurate performance of your techniques.

1. While respecting the adage of "never say never", it is a rare attack that happens in a well-lit, open-spaced, level-floored, fleeing-friendly environment. Attacks happen everywhere and therefore training should not be limited to a mat covered gym or dojo. This is not to say that you should begin your practicing by immediately landing hard falls on pavement or stand on the side of a steep hill to practice your balance, but neither should it exclude these additions to your training. BUILD YOUR TRAINING SLOWLY, but don't allow yourself to hide from difficulty. Train outdoors, in all elements, and at night when visibility is very low or absent.

2. Your training partners may be your friends, but they are not there to make you feel good. When you are practicing the following exercises outlined within this chapter,

do not allow anyone to "let you win". Start off slowly, but make certain to build your training to a credible level. Take time to concentrate on any particular parts of movements that you may be finding problematic until a resolution of your difficulty can be found. Remove all sticking points and do your best to get to the place where you can instruct your team to make the implementation of your training as difficult for you as possible, therefore creating a realistic environment in which you can practice your techniques. Perform your movements over and over again until you can do each without fail, then do it again, and then again. You must be willing to learn and to fail during training, taking one small step at a time until the techniques are finely honed and performed without difficulty. Expertise takes time and only once a practice is executed multiple times will it be ready for actual usage.

3. With the above stated, you must be able to trust your training partners. There is never a need to put yourself or anyone else at risk while practicing. Until expertise is achieved, problems may occur. During training, anyone must be allowed to "tap out." This declaration is the immediate demand to stop all action. Even if physical contact is not present, everything within the training cycle ceases. The most common auditory expression in all martial arts is by simply shouting out: "Tap! Tap!" or simply tapping twice or more upon the ground, yourself, or your attacker. Once it's called, everything stops until everyone present is prepared to resume the training.

4. Not all problems demand a tap out. Consider that if at first you don't succeed, KEEP MOVING!!! Do not waste the golden opportunity of having to reassess and reevaluate a crisis when you are training. Moves don't always work and thinking "on the fly" is an asset that cannot be overstated. If a certain technique or method does not work right away, do not feel the need to always reset and try the same technique again. Try to immediately imagine what you would do from your new position. You won't get to stop and restart in a real crisis, so don't train like you do. Have your partners keep coming at you until an escape is made or someone calls the fight. Take every chance to make your training as realistic as possible.

5. If possible, practice with multiple, random-sized individuals and allow your training to be altered. Create different scenarios to overcome such as trying the same techniques from different angles or changed positions. Regularly increase the level of difficulty. For example, attempt a technique on one knee or try to perform it on the ground. Make it hard for yourself so that no one else may.

6. Survival in a crisis is just as much mental preparation as it is physical. Use the everyday as your practice. Allow yourself to often take a quick moment to analyze your surroundings. You can train yourself quite successfully by scrutinizing any random building, street, or arbitrary environment that you enter into. There does not need to be present danger for you to consider the lay of your surroundings. It is not that danger might occur, but rather that your preparedness is present even when peril lays

dormant. This kind of mental practice will train you to utilize your surroundings in your every day life.

7. **You are not trying to win, you are trying to learn.** Physical contact may not always be needed. Practice the evasions outlined below attempting to restrict as much of the engagement as possible. You may have to perform some techniques to achieve your initial freedom, but do not try to conquer the situation, your job is only to escape it. Remember, it is often said that 99% of martial arts, as well as crisis management, is in the mind. Never forget that if you use your head first, you may not have to use your hands at all.

Physical Training and Practice Sequences

The above section should illuminate the concept that the best defensive training of kung fu is that which attempts to avoid physical contact altogether. However, while respecting the aspects of mental preparation, it is now important to concentrate on the fact that this is not always possible and we must ready ourselves physically for the possibility of a crisis as well. Muscle memory is a concept that our bodies, with proper practice and when placed into a specific circumstance, will perform a pre-chosen action, independent of cognizant thought.

Consider those who suffer from the affliction of sleepwalking. It is a very common occurrence for these persons to rise and accurately perform a myriad of ordinary, daily tasks, regardless of being unconscious. The cause of somnambulism is not the focus here, but rather the effect. People need not be aware of their actions to execute them and each time you practice a technique, your body is memorizing a pattern of movement.

Think about something as easy as signing your name. It is a rare person indeed who needs to concentrate on such a mundane, frequent action. The point is that with proper preparation, you will not need to consider the best action. Indeed, the eventual goal in repetitious training is that your body will eventually sense the situation better than your mind could and subsequently it may choose the most suitable course for you to take. Observe the following training techniques.

Solo Training Drills

Solo Forward Roll Training

Stand forward, leaving ample space in front of you.

Arch your fingers and wrist downward.

Lay the backs of your fingers against the ground.

Create a wheel of your body as you lay your shoulder to the ground.

Complete the technique by laying your feet out ahead of you.

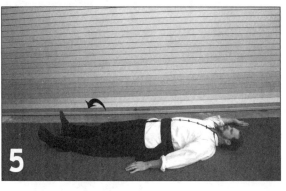

Solo Backward Roll Training

Stand forward, leaving ample space behind you.

Lay the outside of your foot against the ground behind you.

Letting your weight begin to drop in reverse, allow your knee to find itself to the ground.

Create a wheel of your body as you lay your backside to the ground.

Complete the technique by laying your arms out above of you.

Solo Rollover Training

Lay face down upon the ground.

Begin to rotate both your shoulders and hips, thus allowing your lower hand and lower leg to slip underneath.

Complete the technique by sprawling your limbs outward.

Single Attacker Drills

Throat Grab Drill

Allow your partner to grab you by the neck.

Lift your mirror side hand around the outside of the grab.

Grab the base of your partner's thumb, pressing the wrist down to your chest.

To complete the technique, pull the thumb away from you as you rotate your hips and shoulders in the opposite direction.

Single Rising Quick Change Drill

Have your partner grab you over the wrist.

Angle your fingers up toward the constraining wrist.

Arch your hand forward and up, thus stealing the grab.

Single Descending Quick Change Drill

Have your partner grab you under the wrist.

Angle your fingers down toward the constraining wrist.

Arch your hand forward and down, thus stealing the grab.

Single Punch Release Drill

Have your partner grab you by the wrist.

After a firm grip is place over you, simply punch forward to the empty space over your partner's shoulder. This motion will be too much to allow the thumb to maintain the grasp.

Single "Cross-Handed" Snake-Up-The-Branch Training Drill

Have your partner grab you from over the wrist.

Circle your hand upward and to the outside of the grab.

Continuing the circular movement, begin to raise your hand over the top of the grab.

Once gravity is on your side, swing down over the partner's arm.

Finish the movement by completing the circle. This action will easily release you from the grab.

Double-Handed Punch Release Drill

Have your partner grab you by the wrist with both hands.

Begin to point the constrained hand toward the empty space above the partner's shoulder.

Punch straight forward to break the hold that has been placed over you. The pressure will be too great a force for your partner's thumbs to maintain the grab.

Single "Mirror-Handed" Snake-Up-The-Branch Training Drill

Have your partner grab you from on top of your wrist.

Begin to raise your hand in a circular motion around the outside of your partner's hold.

After you rise above his hand, begin to allow gravity to lower your hand down.

Finish the move by forcing the grip placed over you to be removed completely.

Single Elbow Roll Training Drill

Have your partner grab you from over your wrist.

Bring the tip of your constrained elbow up and around the outside of your partner's wrist.

Begin to hook the tip of your elbow over his arm.

Once on top, use your arm like a lever, pulling down and in with your elbow and pressing forward and up with your hand. This action will completely release the hold placed over you.

Paired and Single Directional Movement Drill

Stand ready.

Stand ready.

Begin raising your arm upward to the outside of your partner's arm.

Begin raising your arm in an upward motion.

Making sure to continuously move forward, turn your hand over, facing your palm to the ground.

Making sure to continuously move forward, turn your hand over, facing your palm to the ground.

Begin to arc your forward movement downward over your partner's neck.

Begin to arc your forward movement downward.

Finish by driving your force fully down forcing your partner to the ground.

Finish by driving your force fully down.

Paired Attacker Drills

Double Rising Quick Change Drill (Single Hand Grabs)

Begin by having two partners take hold of both of your wrists with one hand each.

Open your first hand, and slightly bend the wrist upward.

By rising quickly, your partner's thumb will not be able to maintain the hold and you will easily be able to capture the first controlling wrist.

Once free from the first hold, turn your remaining, captured hand upward in the same fashion.

Rise quickly, just as you have previously done on the other side.

Once the drill is complete, you will find yourself in possession of both of your partners' wrists.

Double Descending Quick Change Drill (Single Hand Grabs)

Begin by having two partners grab you by the wrist with one hand each as as your hands are held high.

Open your first hand wide and begin angling it downward, as if to take hold over the constraining hand.

With slight downward pressure, you will break free of your first partner's ability to maintain the hold over you.

Once free of the first hold, angle your still constrained hand downward in the same fashion as the first.

Once again, you will find that with only a bit of well-placed and slight downward pressure, the second partner's wrist will come easily under your control.

The technique is complete once you have taken control of both of your partners' wrists.

Double Elbow Roll Drill (Single Hand Grabs)

Begin by having two partners take hold of both of your wrists with one hand each.

Pulling the captured wrist toward your own stomach, begin to bring the tip of your first elbow over and across the wrist of the partner holding you.

Using the pressure as a lever, pull up on your own wrist and continue the same downward motion with your elbow.

With only slight torsion, your captured arm will break free.

Repeating on the other side, bring the tip of your elbow over and across the wrist of the partner holding you.

Performing the same lever action with your still captured hand, pull up on your wrist while continuing to add downward pressure with your elbow.

Having repeated the same actions of both sides, you will find that you may break free of these types of grabs at your leisure.

Double Forward Rolling Snake-Up-The-Branch Wrist Drill (Single Hand Grabs)

Begin by having two partners take hold of both of your wrists with one hand each.

Circle your first wrist around the outside of the partner to your right.

Continue the movement fully around and over his arm.

After throwing your hand downward to fully release the grab, turn next to the second partner at your left and begin rotating your wrist upward and around the outside of his hold.

Holding your right arm down now, continue the movement of your left arm fully around and over the second partner's grasp.

Continue the movement until your second arm is free.

With slight torsion and continued movement, you will find that you can easily break free of the holds.

Forward Rolling Arm Drill (Double Hand Grabs)

Begin by having two partners take hold of both of your arms.

Circle your first arm around the hold and to the outside of the partner to your right.

Continue the movement fully around and over his arm.

After throwing your hand forward to fully release the grab, turn next to the second partner at your left and begin rotating your arm upward and around the outside of his hold.

Holding your right arm down now, continue the movement of your left arm fully around and over the second partner's grasp.

Continue the movement until your second arm is free.

With slight torsion and continued movement, you will find that you can easily break free of the holds.

Mixed Directional Wrist Roll Drill (Double Hand Grabs)

Begin by having two partners take your wrists with both hands.

Start your movement by rising the captured wrist on your right forward and up away from you.

Once that movement has commenced, begin to swing your left wrist upward in the opposite direction.

Using the two circling motions, rise and roll over the partner on your right and forward press over the wrist of your partner on the left.

Once the hold has been lost by the partner on your left, turn to concentrate on the hold maintained by the partner on your right.

Circle down and over the remaining constraint.

With slight torsion and continued movement, you will find that you can easily break free of the holds.

Double Punch Release Drill (Double Hand Grabs)

Begin by having two partners hold you with both hands at the wrist.

Use one of your captured wrists to attempt to strike over the area at your first partner's shoulder.

Continue to move forward and the rising pressure will be more than the hold of his thumbs may maintain, thus freeing your arm.

Once free of the first partner, turn to face the second.

Utilizing the same forward/rising motion, strike at the empty area over his shoulder, freeing your wrist and releasing you from the hold.

Environmental Escape Drills & Flash Tactics

The idea behind these drills is to remove the standard, predictable routine of training and to keep it to a more random, unexpected, and realistic approach. If possible during this type of training, have a third partner present to assist you. Have them call out commands such as "Left", "Right", or "Center", forcing you to move a certain, perhaps more difficult way. Also one of the most helpful things this third partner can do is to man the light switch. Why? In truth, one of the best ways to train these tactics is to try the drills in a dark room and suddenly have the third partner turn on the lights, leaving you only a mere moment to speculate on the proper path before you have to act.

Two-Man "Run Through" Training Drills

For clarification of the following exercises, the partners in the drills will be referred to as partner #1 and partner #2. (seen above)

Center Breach Drill

Two partners stand in front of you, blocking your desired path.

As your partners approach, you decide to take the center route between them and take the partner #1 by the wrist.

Pulling backward, use the force of the movement to throw partner #1 behind you and project yourself past partner #2 by raising your arm from underneath his hold.

Spin yourself around to allow the full forward force of the two collide.

Once free of their containment, make your way toward the exit.

Left Side Evasion

Two partners stand in front of you, blocking your desired path.

As your partners approach, you decide to take the left route around them.

As they reach your immediate area, take the outside arm of partner #1 and begin to move yourself to the left and out of the way of the dual advancement.

Pulling backward, use the force of the movement to throw partner #1 behind you and spin yourself quickly around to the left side.

Once free of their containment, make your way toward the exit.

Right Side Evasion

Two partners stand in front of you, blocking your desired path.

As your partners approach, you decide to take the right route around them.

As they reach your immediate area, take the outside arm of partner #2 and begin to move yourself to the right and out of the way of the dual advancement.

Pulling backward, use the force of the movement to throw partner #2 behind you and project yourself quickly around to the side.

Once free of their containment, make your way toward the exit.

Mixed Front/Back Evasion

Two partners stand around you, one at your front and one at your back.

As the partners approach, you veer quickly to the side and out of the direct path of their momentum.

Unable to stop themselves, the partners will collide forward into each other, allowing you to spin toward your escape.

Once free of their containment, make your way toward the exit.

Weapon Avoidance Drills

As was mentioned before in Chapter 5, practicing movements with a rubber knife is a wonderful way to recognize points of danger as well as to show direction of movement. However, it is imperative that you NEVER, under any circumstances, train with a real weapon. No matter how realistic you wish to be, the dangers involved will be too great.

Circular Redirection Training Drill

You partner approaches you with a rubber knife.

Using the back of your cross hand, skew the direction of the knife's path upward and away by pressing against the outside of your partner's wrist.

Once the knife is slightly raised, quickly join your free hand underneath to both add support and also to begin the rotation process.

Commence the new rotation to bring the knife downward in a circular fashion.

Make certain to control the knife to its furthest extent as you continue to rotate the attacking arm downward.

Continue manipulating the revolution by controlling the knife to travel between the two of you.

Once it has risen to its furthest point to the far side, allow your initial hand to resume control.

After the knife has returned the beginning upward point, the circle will have been made complete.

Once you have returned the knife to its initial position, you may stop and restart the drill or simply continue the manipulation again.

Chapter Summary

As far as practicing and utilizing the methods and tactics in this book, try to consider that they are not highly distinct pieces of a puzzle that can only be constructed together in one way, but rather methods that should be thought of as complementary shapes. They can be brought together in whichever manner the situation demands. Remember that each of these patterns can be used in any order and may be combined to the preference of the user.

Conclusion

Martial arts are not magic, they are sciences of self defense. They are also your best bet and the fact is well remembered that within survivalist tactics, your job is not to conquer the situation, but rather escape it. That being said, have no regret on what you must do. Sadly, crisis situations occur all the time. You must realize that when the time arises, it is a necessity that you ensure your own safety. The need to utilize the methods that you will use to secure that end, however extreme, was forced upon you. To act properly, you must act completely. Do not feel the need to hold back. It may be difficult not to temper your own ability during a confrontation, but remember that this is always a mistake. Consider *choosing* your actions by the following:

To be placed into a crisis, you were not given a choice to stem the extremes of your attacker. It follows that you therefore do not need to consider this choice yourself. There is no need to think about it other than that. You job is simply to do what you must that you might free yourself from the situation and do not regret it.

Be confident, be determined and never forget that the overriding answer to every question in a crisis situation is the same: Get out and do whatever it takes to survive.

About the Author

Sifu Noah Knapp is a second generation instructor with over a quarter of a century experience in self defense and martial arts. He maintains a third degree black sash in Kung Fu and has extensive training and/or teaching ranks in several other arts such as Kenpo, Karate, Aikido, Kali, Silat & Tai Chi. For over a decade he has served as the head teacher for his family's Kung Fu school as well as outsourcing his instruction to both military and civilian police officers. He may be contacted at sifunoah@yahoo.com

Also Available from Turtle Press:
Fight Back
Winning on the Mat
Wrestle and Win
Fighting the Pain Resistant Attacker
Total Defense
Conditioning for Combat Sports
Kung Fu Grappling
Street Stoppers:
Sendo-Ryu Karate-do
Power Breathing
Throws and Takedowns
Drills for Grapplers
Vital Point Strikes
Groundfighting Pins and Breakdowns
Defensive Tactics
Secrets of Unarmed Gun Defenses
Point Blank Gun Defenses
Security Operations
Vital Leglocks
Boxing: Advanced Tactics and Strategies
Grappler's Guide to Strangles and Chokes
Fighter's Fact Book 2
The Armlock Encyclopedia
Championship Sambo
Complete Taekwondo Poomse
Martial Arts Injury Care and Prevention
Timing for Martial Arts
Strength and Power Training
Complete Kickboxing
Ultimate Flexibility
Boxing: A 12 Week Course
The Fighter's Body: An Owner's Manual
The Science of Takedowns, Throws and Grappling for Self-defense
Fighting Science
Martial Arts Instructor's Desk Reference
Solo Training
Solo Training 2
Fighter's Fact Book
Conceptual Self-defense
Martial Arts After 40
Warrior Speed
The Martial Arts Training Diary for Kids
Teaching Martial Arts
Combat Strategy
The Art of Harmony
Total MindBody Training
1,001 Ways to Motivate Yourself and Others
Ultimate Fitness through Martial Arts
Taekwondo Kyorugi: Olympic Style Sparring
Taekwondo Self-defense
Taekwondo Step Sparring
Complete Kicking

For more information:
Turtle Press
1-800-778-8785
e-mail: orders@turtlepress.com

http://www.turtlepress.com